Teleselling

Wiley Self-Teaching Guides teach practical skills from accounting to astronomy, management to mathematics. Look for them at your local bookstore.

Teleselling

A Self-Teaching Guide

Second Edition

James D. Porterfield

John Wiley & Sons, Inc.

New York • Chichester • Brisbane • Toronto • Singapore

Word list on pages 148–149: From *Power Selling by Telephone* courtesy of Barry Z. Masser of Leadflow, Inc. (Lynwood, Washington) and William M. Leeds of The Leeds Company (Westlake Village, California).

This text is printed on acid-free paper.

This publication is designed to provide accurate and authoritative information in regard to the subject matter covered. It is sold with the understanding that the publisher is not engaged in rendering professional services. If legal, accounting, medical, psychological, or any other expert assistance is required, the services of a competent professional person should be sought.

Library of Congress Cataloging-in-Publication Data:

Porterfield, James D.
    Teleselling : a self-teaching guide / James D. Porterfield.—2nd ed.
      p.   cm.
    Rev. ed. of: Selling on the phone. © 1985.
    Includes bibliographical references (p. 207) and index.
    ISBN 0-471-11567-3 (alk. paper)
    1. Telephone selling.   I. Porterfield, James D.   Selling on the
phone.   II. Title.
HF5438.3.P67   1996
658.8'5—dc20   95-38849

10 9 8 7 6 5 4

To my father, Orville L. Porterfield,
in appreciation for his faith in me

Contents

Preface xi

Acknowledgments xv

Introduction   **1**

Selling on the Phone: A Skills and Attitude Survey 4

1 Using the Telephone to Sell   **8**

Why Use the Telephone to Sell? 8
Where to Use the Telephone to Sell 12
What Does It Take to Sell by Telephone? 15

**2 Buying Motives and Product Benefits:
    The Critical Connection**   **19**

How People Reach a Buying Decision 19
Why People Buy 22
Applying Product Knowledge 27

3 A Basic Sales-Call Strategy   **35**

The Only True Secret of Selling: The Call Flow 35
How to Influence Your Prospective Customer 39
Call Strategy and the Purpose of the Call 43

4 Prospecting   **48**

Knowing Whom to Call 48
Precall Research 53
Prospecting Strategies 54
Special Activity: Getting on the Telephone 61

5 Approach   **62**

Why Grab the Prospect's Attention? 62
Getting a Prospect's Undivided Attention 64
Creating Your Own Attention-Grabbers 67

6 Analyze   **69**

Why Analyze Needs? 69
How to Analyze Needs 72
What Do You Need to Know? 77

7 Advocate   **81**

Advocate Extemporaneously 81
The Elements of a Planned Presentation 83
Advocating the Appropriate Product 85

8 Answer   **91**

The Challenge of Objections 91
Making Objections into Questions You Can Answer 98
And What about the Price Objection? 101

9 Ask   **104**

The Closing Process 104
When to Ask for the Order 105
How to Ask for the Order 108

10 Apply   **114**

Apply Service after the Sale 114
Apply Service to Build Long-Term Relationships 117
Apply Service to Your Customer Responses 121

11 Adapt   **129**

Interacting Positively with People by Telephone 129
The Four Social Styles 131
How to Adapt to Different Personal Styles 135

12 Trouble-Free Telecommunication   **141**

Building Obstacle-Free Communication 141
Using Words That Sell 147

13 Effective Listening   **156**

What Effect Does Listening Have? 156
Are You Listening? 158
Techniques to Improve Your Listening Skills 159

14 Managing Your Calls and Yourself   **165**

Organizing for Success 165
Managing Your Calls 171
Maintaining Your Positive Attitude 176

15 Developing a Script   **182**

The Pros and Cons of Scripted Calls 182
Developing Effective Scripts 185
Two Scripts 188

Performance Evaluation Survey   193

Afterword   197

Appendix A: A Sample Mail-and-Phone Program   199

Appendix B: A Sample Multicall Work Plan   203

Appendix C: Straight A's   206

Sources for More Information   207

Index   211

Preface

This book was written primarily for two distinct groups of readers: individual tellesellers, whether they are beginning work in a marketing organization or seeking to polish their sales skills; and sales representatives and other businesspeople who want to use the telephone to increase their sales productivity. As a result of these two focuses, you may come across information that is applicable only to one group or the other. In addition, there is the occasional discussion of management decisions that might be beyond your authority as a member of a selling staff. But because such decisions can affect your work regardless of the group of readers to which you belong and because many progressive marketing organizations welcome suggestions for improved operations from staff members, I have chosen to include these in the text. All members of a sales team can benefit from a full understanding of the total telemarketing operation, from overall management concerns to daily teleselling sessions.

For you to get full value for the time you spend using *Teleselling: A Self-Teaching Guide,* you should keep these of my opinions and beliefs in mind:

1. *Selling is more art than science.*   For this reason, you *won't* find such magic formulas as "the seven keys to grabbing attention in every call," "the eight secrets to closing a sale," or "fourteen steps to making a million dollars in sales in three weeks." If you fall for such formulas, master the secrets offered, and then fail to accomplish what was promised, you will blame yourself for the failure. Truth is, nobody closes every call they make by getting an order, and no tellesellers, to my knowledge, make a million dollars. A more realistic goal for you to set for yourself

as you work through this book is to increase the frequency of closed sales in your calls.

To enable you to close more sales, you *will* find suggestions, outlines, and forms to help you develop a natural teleselling style that is based on your own strengths and abilities. Upon completion of the book, you will have developed the basic skills needed to be the unique teleseller only you can be and to be successful at your work.

2. *You learn more by doing than by reading how others do.* As a sales manager, sales trainer, and seminar instructor, I adhere to this principle with excellent results. You will see the philosophy reflected here in several ways:

- As a well-motivated, mature professional, working (perhaps out of necessity) with an eye to both job and financial satisfaction, you want to do the best you can. Your motivation and drive will enable you to learn what works for you by training yourself (the reason self-teaching guides exist) rather than by being hand-led through some other person's way of working.

- There are very few teleselling scripts or contrived sales dialogues in the body of this book. Instead, suggested sales phraseology is provided throughout, in order to start you thinking about what you want to say in the situations you encounter. For ultimately it falls on you to develop your scripts or outlines for extemporaneous calls, to try them out, and to revise them as needed to make them work for you. That is how it will be in your work; this book merely starts you in that direction.

- Special Activity: Getting on the Telephone on page 61 is intended to begin this self-teaching process for you. It may appear contradictory to urge you throughout this book to plan both your calls and what you are going to say once you are on the telephone, and then to have you spend a day on the telephone before you begin the skill-building section of the book. However, I am convinced that the benefit to you of completing the Special Activity outweighs the example it sets. The activity will set in your mind, more than any urging, why the remainder of the book is important.

3. *Keep it simple.* Woody Hayes, legendary football coach at Ohio State University, taught his players that "if you get fancy, you get beat." For you as a teleseller, this means:

- Keep your goals simple and attainable.

- Keep your product choices for the prospect simple and understandable.

- Keep your selling message simple and to the point.

To the extent you are able to do this, you will win the undying gratitude, not to mention the business, of your customers and prospects.

One final note: The telephone can be used to sell all manner of goods and services, from encyclopedias to office decoration and maintenance services. For the sake of word economy, though, throughout the book I refer to both goods and services as products. When you read "product," you can substitute "goods" or "services" and not change the application or meaning.

Acknowledgments

There are several people who were instrumental in my learning and applying the material presented here. I would first like to thank Robert Farkas, who helped me go from failure to success in selling. Thanks also to Dick Bryant, who first described for me the potential of "selling on the phone" and who set me on the right track as a teleselling training consultant. To John Ferraro, owner of Corporate Management Systems, Inc., who encouraged me to convert what I know into a successful seminar. To my editor Judith McCarthy at John Wiley & Sons who, with the patience of a saint, urged the project to completion; to Judy Cardanha, the copyeditor, who turned the manuscript around with speed and understanding. And to the reviewers of the first edition, whose valuable input resulted in a successful book: Mary Ann Kroop, Franklin Kavaler, Allen Simeone, E. Jack Pudney, Gail Cohen, Tom Stanton, Harold Brown, Al Pratico, Diane Loucks, Eileen Hauptman, Martha Trexler, Virginia McNeill, Mark J. Heller, Regina Quartararo, and Bernard Cohen.

Introduction

Either you or the company for which you work has elected to use an exciting and challenging selling medium: the telephone. Using the telephone as a way of selling is a recent phenomenon, and your decision to join this movement means that you will have to learn a number of new skills. But a reminder before you start: Using the telephone changes only one aspect of your selling work—the *method* of delivering your sales message. To place yourself in front of prospects and customers, you will use a telephone instead of an automobile and your legs. Otherwise, while certain skills take on added emphasis, the selling process and the basic skills shared by salespeople everywhere have not been changed.

In order for you to succeed at teleselling, three things are required of you. First, you must be well versed in basic selling skills, the techniques you employ day in and day out while doing your job. Second, you must know your products inside out. Third, you must communicate what you know in a manner that gets sales. This book has been written to help you equip yourself with these needed techniques and skills. Its goal is to enable you to become a successful professional teleseller.

If you are an experienced salesperson who is just beginning to sell by telephone, you will still benefit from following this book from start to finish. The transition from outside sales to teleselling will require some adaptation on your part. The skills and abilities needed in both fields are the same, but certain skills take on increased importance in telephone selling.

Teleselling is designed to be a complete basic course in selling by telephone. To gain maximum benefit from your work with it, the following procedures will prove helpful:

1. Read the Contents. It outlines the chapters and gives you a brief introduction to all the skills needed to be successful as a teleseller.

2. Leaf through the book and read the Key that appears at the start of each chapter. These Keys give you a minicourse in the basics of teleselling and set up for you an overview of the teleselling process and your role in it.

3. Complete the Skills and Attitude Survey on page 4, including the goal-setting portion. Instructions for interpreting your survey results are found at its conclusion. If you are new to selling and teleselling, this activity will sharpen your focus on the skills and attitudes needed for success. If you are an experienced salesperson, it will identify those areas where you may need to adapt your behavior to selling by telephone.

4. Read Chapter 1 and each succeeding chapter in order. You are strongly urged to *complete all activities* within each chapter as you come to them.

5. Complete the activities posed in On Your Own at the end of each chapter. Your successful completion of each one signals your readiness to move on to the next chapter.

6. At the conclusion of each chapter, complete the Self-Inventory. It will help you access your strengths and weaknesses and check your understanding of the chapter. The correct answer to each of these statements is "yes." Those statements to which your instinct tells you to respond "no" identify the areas for which you need to concentrate on improving your skills. Go back and reread the relevant part of the chapter.

7. Begin working on the telephone as soon as possible. The Special Activity at the end of Chapter 4 applies the "learn by doing" principle and lets both the book and your experience be your teacher. The world is full of prospects, more than you will ever be able to contact. If you treat them courteously, most are forgiving should you have to contact them again later when you are more effective.

8. Complete the Performance Evaluation Survey on page 193. Instructions on how to score the Survey are found in its opening paragraph. This Survey provides a method by which you can, either point by point or taking your overall performance into consideration, compare how you feel about needed skills and attitudes and how well you do when you perform or apply them.

9. When you have completed this book and its concluding Performance Evaluation Survey, do not think you are finished with it. Come back to both the Self-Inventories and the Survey occasionally and redo them. Compare your new results with your old ones to measure your improved skills and attitudes toward your work. Over time, you should see an increasing number of "yes" answers in your Self-Inventories. You should also see increasingly corresponding numbers, both for individual items and in total, when looking at the "Importance" and "Level of Performance" scores in your Performance Evaluation Survey.

10. Begin a lifelong professional reading program, as recommended in the Afterword. Sources for More Information, on page 207, is a starting point. Also find suggestions at several locations in the book on how you can keep up your reading program.

Note to Training Professionals: There is a free Conference Leaders Guide available to accompany *Teleselling, A Self-Teaching Guide, Second Edition.* It offers suggestions, activities, and additional materials for using this book in a training environment, including outlines for employing its content in both one-day (two-session) and two-day (four-session) programs. To request your free copy of this guide, write to:

STG Editor
John Wiley & Sons, Inc.
Professional & Trade Division
605 Third Avenue
New York, NY 10158-0012

SELLING ON THE PHONE: A SKILLS AND ATTITUDE SURVEY

As you answer the following questions, feel free, where appropriate, to comment beyond a simple "yes" or "no" (see suggestions for interpreting the Survey at its conclusion). Consider your answers as you set at least three goals for yourself to guide your work through the chapters that follow. These goals should reflect your motives for picking up this book in the first place.

1. Do I have a call plan before I pick up the telephone?

   ____

   ____

2. Can I distinguish between a product's characteristics or features, the resulting advantages, and the benefits a prospect might derive from them? Which do I emphasize—features, advantages, or benefits?

   ____

   ____

3. Do I have a selling strategy I employ in each telephone call I handle?

   ____

   ____

4. Do I handle my calls in a manner that inspires confidence in me and in the way my company is managed?

   ____

   ____

5. Do I spend my time on the telephone wisely, talking to high-priority prospects who are ready to make a buying decision?

   ____

   ____

6. Do I gain and keep my prospect's attention throughout the call?

   _____

   _____

7. Do I determine a prospect's wants or needs before I try to sell my product?

   _____

   _____

8. Am I attentive to what my prospect says, or do I have to ask the prospect to repeat things?

   _____

   _____

9. Do I always deliver a well-thought-out, logical selling message?

   _____

   _____

10. Do my prospects hear and comprehend what I say to them?

    _____

    _____

11. Do my prospects understand me, or do they occasionally ask me to explain what I mean?

    _____

    _____

12. What major objections to buying do I encounter?

    _____

    _____

13. How, and how well, do I answer the objections I encounter?

_____

_____

14. Before ending the conversation, do I ask the prospect to take the action that was the goal of my call?

_____

_____

15. Do I follow up on every closed sale to ensure the customer's complete satisfaction?

_____

_____

16. Do I adjust my behavior to react in the most positive way to the various personality types I encounter on the telephone?

_____

_____

17. Do I handle rejection well enough so that it doesn't discourage me?

_____

_____

18. What obstacles do I encounter that interfere with my ability to communicate effectively with my prospects?

_____

_____

19. Do my teleselling conversations average no more than five minutes per call?

_____

_____

20. Am I contacting an average of ten decision-makers during each hour I am on the telephone?

_____

_____

My goals for improving my teleselling technique are:

1. _____

_____

_____

_____

2. _____

_____

_____

_____

3. _____

_____

_____

_____

A fully trained and successful teleseller would want to be able to answer "yes" to each of the twenty questions. As you review your answers make note of any question to which you responded "no" or that made you hedge or qualify your answer (i.e., "Well, no, but . . ." or "I'm not sure that applies to me"). Those questions point to areas about which you want to be especially concerned. Furthermore, the areas of weakness highlighted by a "no" answer should be your primary concern when setting goals for improving your teleselling technique.

1 Using the Telephone to Sell

THE KEY

The telephone is a powerful tool for salespeople. It easily and inexpensively brings them into contact with prospective and existing customers. Regardless of the purpose of that contact—cold calling to find prospects, qualifying prospects, making appointments, closing sales, or providing after-the-sale service—the telephone is used to conduct all the same business that an outside salesperson does. This chapter discusses the benefits of teleselling, outlines the many ways teleselling can apply to your work in sales, and identifies skills that tellers share with face-to-face salespeople as well as skills that, if not unique, certainly take on greater importance for tellers.

WHY USE THE TELEPHONE TO SELL?

The technology that makes a book like this one useful to a large number of people was put into service less than thirty years ago. Since then, a number of other factors have contributed to making teleselling an attractive alternative to the more established sales channels. The result is that today the telephone has changed forever the way all things are sold.

Telephone Technology

The first call using a WATS (Wide Area Telephone Service) line was made in 1967. Popular historians may not rank this with Alexander Graham Bell's

"Mr. Watson, come here. I want you!" But the enormous ramifications of the event dwarf the importance of what was said. Outbound WATS enables the placing of long-distance calls at a fixed rate, rather than at the more expensive per-call cost. Combined with inbound WATS (1-800 service), low-cost and large-scale use of the telephone by businesses, even over large geographic areas, has become a reality.

Today, technology that allows easy, inexpensive, and fast access to virtually all markets is at hand. Examples include:

- Random dialers, which automatically dial each number in an exchange, then play a recorded message to the answering party. A message to qualified prospects, for example, can end with instructions either to stay on the line to speak with a teleseller or to leave an acknowledgment that will initiate a callback.

- Call-routing equipment, common in larger telemarketing operations, which automatically routes a call through the various long-distance services to which the user subscribes (e.g., AT&T, Sprint, or MCI) and places it on the least expensive line available at the moment.

- Caller identification technology, which enables a company to identify calls coming from a specific area code, then routes the calls to telesellers specially trained in the products currently being marketed in that area.

Credit Cards and Computers

Two other developments have also influenced the rapid growth of telemarketing. The use of universal credit cards (e.g., MasterCard, Visa, American Express, Discover Card, and the like) has made it possible for consumers to purchase and receive goods and services anywhere in the world. Meanwhile, personal computers, coupled with sophisticated database software, now enable marketers to capture, cross-reference, and call up information on consumers' buying behavior and location with merely a few keystrokes.

There is a rapidly expanding market for telecommunications hardware, software, and financial services, all of which lower costs and improve productivity. The competition among supplying companies to meet the demand has made sophisticated technology available to even the smallest user of telemarketing. The result has been the emergence of telemarketing as a major component of a company's selling effort. The Direct Marketing Association reports that, in a recent year, 55.2 percent of America's adult population ordered merchandise by mail or phone, with telemarketing alone generating an estimated $280 billion in sales, and the nation's approximately 1.3 million toll-free (800) telephone numbers received 11.7 billion calls from consumers.

The use of the telephone as a marketing tool is also a consequence of its omnipresence in modern life. Anyone can pick up a telephone and call into 97.5 percent of the homes in America and virtually 100 percent of businesses, generally within a matter of seconds. As a marketer, whether to consumers or to other businesses, you can certainly go more places on a one-to-one basis more quickly and easily by telephone than via any other medium.

Cost Factors

Another factor that makes the telephone an important marketing tool is the high cost of all other selling methods. For instance, although estimates of the actual cost of a single outside sales visit made by a salesperson vary widely, the significant finding is that the cost per visit has increased by as much as 33 percent in the past five years, up to estimated amounts in excess of $300. Equally important, these face-to-face visits can only be cost-effective if the prospects are highly likely to buy. It soon becomes clear that the cost of making a sales contact must be reduced.

If you sell outside at present, you can determine your own cost of calls by using Table 1.1. Refer to your expense records so the numbers will be as accurate as possible. If you already work as a teleseller for a company that has outside salespeople and you want to compare your performance to theirs, this data might be available from those salespeople or from sales management.

After completing the table, determine how many calls you (or the typical outside-sales representative) made in the past year. Divide that number into the total dollars spent. Your answer is a simple estimate of the cost per call for outside work.

Direct-mail marketing has also experienced cost increases. The Direct Marketing Association reports that the cost of a relatively simple direct-mail package aimed at 250,000 prospects has nearly doubled in the past ten years—postal rates alone went up 25 percent in 1991. And despite increasingly sophisticated mailing-list management and selection techniques, there has been little improvement in the overall 1 to 2 percent response rate. At today's prices, the cost for a typical large mailing (100,000 pieces) can be between $500 and $750 per thousand. With a 1 percent response rate (ten out of the thousand), that makes the cost of one sale $50 to $75. And not all products lend themselves to direct-mail selling exclusively.

Selling by telephone has a price, too. In addition to salaries, rent, furniture,

TABLE 1.1.   OUTSIDE SALES REPRESENTATIVE EXPENSES

Item	Past year	This year
Automobile purchase		
Automobile operation		
Fuel		
Tolls/Fares		
Parking		
Maintenance		
Taxis		
Air/Rail travel		
Lodging		
Entertainment		
Salary		
Totals		
Comments		

supplies, and other expenses associated with operating an office, there is the cost of acquiring telephone directories or mailing lists that include telephone numbers and, of course, the special equipment and long-distance services required. But even so, experience has shown that, at the rate of one sale for ten completed calls to those you suspect might buy, even moderate-sized telemarketing operations can realize a cost-of-sale as low as $10 per order.

Saving Time

Today, companies face increasingly stiff competition for consumer dollars. Shoppers have a wide selection of products and suppliers, which makes it likely that they will search for the best buy. As a result, marketers find it necessary to work smarter and make the most of the finite number of hours in which to get their message out and close a sale. Telephone sales offer time savings to both the prospect and the teleseller. Many buyers will tell you they prefer to deal with the time-sensitive salesperson who makes some or all sales contact by telephone. It is being increasingly accepted that business-to-business telephone marketing is more effective than face-to-face selling. Consumer marketers, especially catalog marketers and media advertisers who use 800 numbers, continue to report unprecedented results.

The telephone is a uniquely versatile marketing tool. It puts the flexibility to respond to changing needs and/or new situations or product/market mixes literally at your fingertips, without an elaborate retooling of your marketing methods. For example, envision the impact a significant new pricing strategy would have on a sales staff that works outside. First, each salesperson would have to be notified, whether by mail, telephone, or a summons to the home office. Then a lot of time would be expended as the representatives traveled to their customers and prospects to explain the pricing policy, while trying to close additional sales. By contrast, if all tellers work from the same location, all it takes to dispense the information to them is a simple morning meeting. The time it takes for the new policy to affect sales is cut down, too, as tellers can contact their customers and prospects almost immediately. The same new policy could be explained and used to advantage in as little as one day. As a telemarketing operation grows, it will realize an additional benefit: easier, more efficient, and closer supervision of the selling operation.

To help decide your purpose in using teleselling in your company or work, follow these suggestions:

1. List the factors outlined here that prompted you to investigate teleselling as an alternative to your present sales activity.

2. List the telephone's strengths from which you expect to benefit.

3. As specifically as possible, comment on how you plan to benefit from each strength you listed.

WHERE TO USE THE TELEPHONE TO SELL

Once you decide to telesell, you must target areas to call. This decision will vary depending on the product, the company, the teleselling campaign, and the market. To begin, determine what you want to accomplish. Do you plan to use the telephone only for a segment of your selling activity, or will you rely on telemarketing for the entire sales process? Whichever you decide, you should then tailor your application of the telephone to that decision.

Qualifying Leads

There are many applications available to you, but a primary one is the ability to qualify leads. In the broadest sense, a *lead* is anyone in your target market who has expressed a desire to know more about your product(s). Whether your leads are collected as a result of advertising, by direct mail, by a random dialer, from evaluating former or present customers, or from information supplied by a different telemarketing organization, you can use the telephone to qualify them further. You'll want to make sure the person not only needs your product, but will buy now or in the near future, has the available money to buy, and has the authority to make a buying decision.

Follow-up Calls

Even if you qualify leads in some way other than by telephone, the telephone will allow you to follow them up quickly and efficiently for sales action. It is good practice for you to always leave the door open to a follow-up call, and there are several ways to do this: You might call to inquire if the information you sent recently has arrived or to present additional "new" information of interest to the prospect. If your selling cycle is a long one, this might be a planned technique to keep the prospect's interest in your product high.

You can establish telephone contact after some other marketing campaign has been instituted. It is especially effective to combine teleselling with one or more additional marketing activities. A telephone call might follow a direct-mail piece, an advertisement, or a salesperson's visit. The goals for such calls can range from further qualifying leads, to answering objections and closing business. To clarify what those goals are, ask yourself such questions as: Is it reasonable to expect to close a sale in only one call? If further contact is needed, what form should that contact take? Once the goals for your calls are clear, you can plan what you will say.

Supporting Salespeople

Outside salespeople should spend their time on high-priority prospects who are ready to make a buying decision. You can use the telephone to support outside salespeople: Working from a list of qualified prospects, a teleseller can conduct an initial interview, preparing the prospect for a sales call, setting up an appointment, and gathering the information needed to make the salesperson's visit as effective as possible. You can often use the telephone to contact parties who can influence the buying decision but who are hard to reach or inappropriate to see. Telephone support helps outside salespeople to make more calls that produce results, thus reducing your cost of sales.

With someone else providing that telephone support, the outside salesperson has no need to spend days in the office trying to make appointments or wasting time following unproductive leads. She is free to spend 100 percent of her time in face-to-face selling with ready-to-buy prospects. The most important factor in such a system is that the teleseller works cooperatively with the salesperson.

Keeping in Touch

The telephone is especially effective as a means of keeping in touch with existing accounts. The value of keeping a hard-gained customer satisfied cannot be overestimated. You can call when your records indicate the customer's supply of your product or its accessories is running low or when you think, from your knowledge of your market and its buying cycle, a peak need for your product will exist. Similarly, you should review your inactive former accounts and reactivate any of those you can. Call simply because you want to "update your records," but then follow with a presentation of your new products or prices when appropriate. In all cases, if you have a valid reason for calling, you will achieve results. The telephone lets you keep in touch with your customers, provide caring service, and learn of new developments that will enable you to keep your competitive edge. And, you can do all of this effectively, frequently, and inexpensively. Of course, getting orders is the major goal of the teleseller.

To further help you plan your use of telemarketing, fill in Table 1.2.

A Complete Selling Tool

You should not think of your telephone as a second-choice instrument for selling. For many companies, the telephone has become the primary method of selling. It emphatically is not a less-than-perfect substitute for having an outside salesperson call on customers. Telesellers can achieve all that outside salespeople can for their customers and their company. They can establish a presence, build rapport, fill business needs, service and befriend customers, and create an identity and image for their company, their product, and themselves.

In increasing numbers, sales and marketing executives are learning that it is no longer economically practical to market solely through an outside sales staff. The inefficiencies inherent in using such a system exclusively make closing a sale very expensive. Whether you are integrating the telephone into

TABLE 1.2. DETERMINING WHERE AND HOW TO USE THE TELEPHONE

Marketing activity	How presently handled	How teleselling can help	Goal of teleselling	Follow-up activity
Qualify leads				
Produce prospects				
Make appointments				
Gather needed information				
Close sales				
Reactivate inactive accounts				
Sell to low-volume accounts				
Service established accounts				

one or more of the steps in the selling process that apply to your business or are planning to devote the entire process to the telephone, you and your company will experience cost reduction, increased efficiency, greater productivity, and, most important, greater profits.

WHAT DOES IT TAKE TO SELL BY TELEPHONE?

What do a pair of legs, a stamped-and-addressed envelope, an automobile, and a telephone have in common? Give up? Each is a means of putting yourself in front of a prospective customer. Once you are in front of that prospective customer, no matter what means you use, what you say and do to persuade the customer to buy your product is essentially the same. So one requirement for success at teleselling is a knowledge of basic selling skills.

In fact, a definition of *teleselling*, adapted from telemarketing consultant Rudy Oetting's definition of *telemarketing* in the Direct Marketing

Association's Telemarketing Council publication *Telephone Marketing*, reads: "a direct marketing medium through which products or services can be offered or discussed when a combination of *systematic activities* and *telecommunications devices* brings a *trained and prepared human being* into a *tightly controlled dialogue* with *another human being who has been carefully selected* for contact based on characteristics [that] indicate close affinity with those products and services." [italics mine]

The important thing to note in Oetting's definition is that, with one exception, the elements apply to all types of selling effort: face-to-face, direct mail, and teleselling. All of selling is a combination of *systematic activities* carried out by *trained people*, conducted in a *controlled* environment with prospects who have been *carefully selected*. The element unique to teleselling is the medium, the *telecommunications device*.

Skills for All Salespeople

There are other factors common to the work of all salespeople. They are worth noting as you begin to plan greater use of the telephone in sales. They include:

1. *Establishing objectives.*   Your objectives can be expressed as a gross- or net-sales dollar target or as a percent of market share. They can be measurable activities that you know will lead to sales, such as soliciting leads, qualifying prospects, or setting up appointments. Regardless of what your goals are, they should be measurable and realistic.

2. *Establishing and maintaining control over your activity.*   Controls will enable you to determine whether you meet the goals you set. If you see you are falling short, you can then evaluate what adjustments to make.

3. *Knowing and planning for a sales-call flow and product-presentation strategy.*   This is a prescribed or recommended way to get from prospecting to closing. It should include an interview opener, the questions you will ask, a list of likely objections, your answers to those objections, the point at which you will ask for the order, and a decision as to what size order is worth the time needed to close it.

4. *Careful screening to ensure that you are calling on the right prospects.* Before you pick up the telephone, you should know whom you are calling and why.

5. *Knowing your product to be of use and value to its intended market.*

You cannot expect to get very far if even you do not believe in your product.

Skills Particular to Tellsellers

There are additional skills, as well as increased emphasis on some common skills, that are required of those who sell on the phone. Because you are not in the presence of the prospect the words you use, for example, not only have to tell your story but must also fully describe the product and its benefits, enabling the prospect to envision it. Other sales techniques, such as product demonstrations or group selling, are less important or completely inapplicable.

Word usage is but one of the differences between teleselling and face-to-face selling. Other challenges posed by teleselling are:

1. *Time constraints.*   You generally have a shorter time to conduct your sales call.

2. *Use of sales literature.*   Without prior planning, contact, and work, you cannot use printed sales aids. You have to mail them in advance or deliver them later.

3. *Widely scattered contacts.*   You must be prepared to deal with the local problems and prejudices of an audience that can be regional, or even national or international.

4. *Building rapport.*   You must work hard to establish trust and empathy with only a voice—without benefit of a smile and a handshake.

5. *An increased emphasis on listening.*   You must learn to read your prospect's voice because the telephone prohibits other avenues of effective communication, such as observing your customer's body language or the setting and behavior around your prospective customer.

6. *The element of surprise.*   Unlike outside salespeople, who work from a schedule of appointments, you often "drop in" unexpectedly and, therefore, must grab the person's attention away from whatever he or she was doing when you called.

Each of these categories, basic selling skills, adapting to the use of the telephone in selling, and effectively communicating your selling message to people over the telephone, will be covered in the chapters that follow. Before you proceed, however, pause now to set the goals that will guide your work throughout the book and to measure your understanding of this chapter.

Remember, your goal(s) will change depending on whom you are calling. And achieving the goal becomes the "closed sale" you aim for in each call.

ON YOUR OWN

1. Refer back to Table 1.2 and decide which marketing activities you will complete in your teleselling work.

2. What is the goal of your call? (Refer to the "goal" column of Table 1.2.) If you plan to make more than one call to each person, what is the goal of each call?

3. Whom do you plan to call to accomplish your goal(s)? Leads? Qualified prospects? Customers?

		Yes	No
SELF-INVENTORY	1. I know which of my marketing activities will benefit most from teleselling.	____	____
	2. I presently make use of the telephone to conduct some selling activity.	____	____
	3. My use of the telephone in sales is coordinated with other marketing methods.	____	____
	4. My using the telephone for selling is as useful and professional as making face-to-face calls on a prospect or customer.	____	____
	5. I know what results I have to achieve to demonstrate the effectiveness of the telephone in my marketing strategy.	____	____

2 Buying Motives and Product Benefits: The Critical Connection

THE KEY

Customers bring a tangled combination of factors into consideration as they decide whether or not to buy a product. A successful teleseller has to be aware of these factors. Furthermore, you need a full understanding of what motivates a buyer to make a buying decision. Finally, you have to know your products inside and out—how they work, what they are used for, who uses them, what their competitive advantages are, and, most important, what benefits a prospect gains from using them. You then bring all of this knowledge together to show a prospective customer how your products satisfy his or her buying motives. This chapter provides insight into the buyer's decision-making process, challenges you to identify what motivates people to buy from you, and instructs you in how to use your knowledge of your products to meet and satisfy those motivations.

HOW PEOPLE REACH A BUYING DECISION

It is axiomatic in selling that, before a person pulls out her wallet, checkbook, credit card, or purchase order, she has to have a clear and satisfactory answer to the question, "What's in it for me if I make this purchase?" To understand how that question gets answered, come with me as I go shopping for a new car.

My job as an instructor at a large university requires that, three days a week, I drive 3.2 miles to campus. There, I park my car, teach my classes, and then make the 3.2-mile return trip home. Occasional runs to the library, copy shop, business supply store, and post office complete my use of this car. As a result, it accumulates an average of 50 miles a week.

Until now, I have relied on an older car for this local running around. But it recently suffered an irreparable effect of its age that sent me in search of a new car. I narrowed my choices down to two models. The first is a nifty compact. In its five-door (hatchback) model, it offers enough space to transport household goods as well as business materials, would seat my children comfortably, operates at a fuel-efficient 37 miles per gallon, comes in an attractive assortment of colors and with a full range of standard options—such as power brakes and steering, AM/FM stereo cassette player, and dual air bags—and sells at a reasonable "no dicker sticker" price.

The other model under consideration is a luxurious German import. This beauty comes with many of the same features as the compact, but it offers several startlingly different options. These include a leather-and-wood-grained interior and power accessories that customize the car's environment to the various drivers for whom it is programmed. The price is about nine times more than that of the hatchback.

Buying Considerations

What to do, what to do? There are three types of considerations that will influence my final decision on which car to buy:

1. *Rational considerations.* These are objective, quantifiable, and measurable—the factors that most intelligent and informed consumers would agree are important to consider when presented with the same set of buying circumstances. What rational considerations can you identify that would be likely to influence me in my search for a new car? List at least three:

   1. _____

   2. _____

   3. _____

Among the rational factors I might take into account are: whether the car is capable of delivering me an average of 50 miles a week; whether the car can withstand the wear and tear young children will give it; the cost of operating, maintaining, and insuring the car; and certainly the price of each car versus the amount I have budgeted for the purchase.

2. *Emotional considerations.* These result from my sometimes unobjective way of looking at things and from how I feel about what I am buying. Can you list up to three emotional considerations that might enter into my car-buying decision?

1. _____

2. _____

3. _____

Emotional factors might include: an appeal to good taste (I might be the kind of person who has to have the best of everything when I make a purchase), optimism about the future (I might think, "Well, you never know, the next account I retain as a consultant may be 'the big one.' If that happens, I'll get rid of the compact and buy the luxury car anyway. I might as well save myself the trouble and buy the luxury car now"), fear that one car might be more desirable to thieves when it is left parked in a lot for long periods of time, and a fondness for one of the colors in which a car is available.

3. *Rationalizations.* When there is a gap between the rational and emotional factors at work on a buyer, rationalizations come into play. These are self-serving but perhaps inappropriate reasons for making a purchase favored by one's emotions. The larger the gap—certainly the case with my car-buying dilemma—the greater the need for the buyer to rationalize, or compensate for, an emotion-based decision. If I actually buy a luxury car in this situation, I'm going to have some explaining to do—to myself and to my family—over why I spent nine times as much as I had to when buying a new car for work. What reasons might I give to rationalize a decision for the luxury car?

1. _____

2. _____

3. _____

Some rationalizations might be: that, historically, one car holds its value better than the other and sometimes even increases in value, that one car fits my image (well-respected author, famous consultant, teacher at a large and well-known university) better than the other, and that the more expensive car is better built and, thus, will protect me and my family in an accident.

If you decide that a prospect is leaning toward an emotional rather than a rational buying decision and that the gap between the two sets of factors is great enough to jeopardize the sale, you will want to provide the prospect with rationalizations for the decision. (*Note:* This is not meant to urge you to manipulate the buyer into purchasing something he or she does not need. That sort of manipulation is out-of-bounds among professional telesellers. But, because buyers do not always make strictly rational buying decisions, you must be aware of the rationalization process buyers go through when making an emotional decision that is at odds with the rational considerations.)

Making Buying Considerations Work

How does the existence of these three factors affect you? More important, how do you make a sale in light of the buyer's constant evaluation of rational and emotional factors and the possible need for rationalization? To increase the likelihood that you'll make a sale in each call you handle, you have to:

- Learn what the prospect's motives are—both rational and emotional—for making the purchase.

- Present the benefits of your product in such terms that your product satisfies the prospect's motives.

- Help satisfy the need for rationalization when there is gap between the rational and emotional considerations.

WHY PEOPLE BUY

Now that you have looked at the factors prospective buyers take into consideration when making a purchase decision, it is appropriate to look at what motives they might be trying to satisfy with the purchases they make. First, look at yourself for a moment.

- Who are you? It would be safe to bet you are a person who holds one of three positions: sales or telemarketing manager, telephone sales training director, or outside or inside salesperson.

- Why did you buy this book? If you are a sales or telemarketing manager, you might want to encourage (or require, as managers are wont to do) greater or more effective use of the telephone by your people in order to either increase sales or reduce costs—or both.

    If you are a telephone sales training director charged with the responsibility of training telesellers, you might ask, "Why reinvent the wheel? I'll assign this book and use my time to prepare for in-class activities."

    If you are a salesperson or are new to teleselling, you might be eager to get ahead of your peers and competitors or to increase the rewards and satisfaction you receive from your work. As a result, you want to learn to make better use of the telephone in your selling.

These three possible buyers illustrate six motives for buying *Teleselling*. The manager wants to increase sales and reduce costs. The training director wants to save time and be more effective in the classroom. The salesperson wants to increase productivity and get more satisfaction out of the work.

Understanding Motives

The first step toward understanding a buyer's motives is to realize that people buy *benefits*, not *products*. How each buyer benefits will vary from one person to another. So the answer to that all-important question "What's in it for me?" is often complex.

A benefit is what the prospect can expect to gain when he or she buys your product. Here, *gain* refers to the expectations that will be satisfied by the benefits your product offers—the psychological factors that come into play to prompt a person to make a buying decision. Once you have identified the buying motives at work, you will know which of your product's benefits to stress in your sales presentation. For example, your home housecleaners are fully bonded (a product attribute), thereby providing the buyer *convenience* and *peace of mind* (two product benefits). Or, your word-processing equipment can manage five stations simultaneously (one attribute); thus, it *saves money* (one benefit) by increasing productivity. Demonstrating that your product will satisfy the buyer's motives by delivering sought-after benefits will enable you to close the sale.

The second step in your sales-call strategy is to analyze the prospect's needs and desires. Needs are the "must-haves." For example, all law firms *must have* available a law library that is complete and current; all offices *must have* on hand an adequate amount of the necessary supplies to conduct their business. Your job in this situation is to determine which of the must-haves you can satisfy to the benefit of your prospect in order to make the sale.

Desires are the "would-like-to-haves." They are more subtle, and fulfilling them depends more on your selling creativity. For example, a car owner might need to have liability insurance to satisfy the law; but the unique features of your automobile coverage—guaranteed renewal, annual premiums, and claim service that is as near as a telephone—can all help you show the prospect why he *would like to have* yours rather than that of the competition. In this case, you offer added convenience and peace of mind. If you can stress benefits that might not even have occurred to the prospect when considering coverage, you can create a desire to buy.

Tuning in to Motives

Every buying decision, then, whether to satisfy a must-have need or a would-like-to-have desire, is motivated by something. It is, therefore, important to your success that you attune your selling to the buying motivation of each of your prospects.

What are the most common buying motivations? The ones discussed here are at work in most buying situations. Additional motives may be at work on the prospects you call, depending on your product and market.

Financial gain is one of the strongest motives at work on buyers, whether they are individual consumers, professionals buying for business, or key business executives themselves. Financial gain can come from making a purchase that will increase in value, such as real estate or a similar investment. It can come from reducing costs, as when a company buys a faster data-processing system or when an individual purchases a new freezer to save on food costs by buying in bulk. Finally, financial gain can be demonstrated by showing a prospective buyer how your product will increase productivity for her business. Showing your prospect a financial gain from the buying decision that you recommend will almost always elicit a favorable response.

Security, whether physical, emotional, or financial, is another important motivation to buy. A business might spend millions to protect the information stored in its computers from theft or manipulation. Diamonds have been promoted for years as being "forever," thus symbolizing emotional security. People buy insurance so they are protected from the financial damage an unexpected loss can inflict on them. If you can show a prospect how purchasing your product will bring more security to his or her life or business, you will have gone a long way toward closing the sale.

Convenience is important to busy people; it is a very strong buying motivation. Selling by telephone, you are in an excellent position to stress convenience in your sales message, especially when follow-up and service are important to the purchase. Your product, too, can offer convenience. It can be easier to operate, less prone to break down, more certain in its performance, or longer lasting than competing products. The benefits of your product that offer convenience should be emphasized in your sales message from the beginning.

Sex appeal can influence the decision to buy many products. Does a health spa sell physical fitness, sex appeal, or both? Can you tell them apart? Even cigarettes and alcoholic beverages are sold by promoting an image of masculinity or femininity. If you are selling structural steel components to bridge contractors, you might have trouble finding a sexual motive in the buying decision. But if you can find one, use it.

Fear as a motivation has long been used in selling. And it is a complex motive with many ramifications. You should recognize your customer's fears and make them work *for* you. For example, a prospect might question (fear) whether your product is reliable. Another prospect might fear he will look bad to friends or colleagues or might fall behind the competition if he doesn't have a certain product or doesn't make a wise purchase. Still another prospect might be afraid of making a large financial commitment or of buying the wrong thing. The fear of financial setback will motivate some people to invest in extended warranties or service contracts on such consumer goods as cars and appliances. To keep fear from working against you, play up the size, history, and success of your company, as well as your personal and professional qualifications as a teleseller. Give the prospect a list of companies that use your product, whether they are clients of your consulting firm or the Fortune 500 buyers of your company's new office equipment. Such actions are reassuring and quiet subjective fears that may stand in the way of a sale.

Pleasure, meaning "an improvement in the quality of one's work or personal life," can also motivate people to buy. For many people, having the best, latest, or most of something gives them pleasure. For others, knowing a product will increase the satisfaction they derive at work or play will lead to a purchase. This is not to recommend that you overdo the use of superlatives in your sales talk. But you can respond to this motivation by stressing the ways your product will enhance the quality of the prospect's life.

Acceptance and *respect* are strong motivators. Most people want to earn the approval, even the admiration, of their peers, loved ones, or colleagues. Certainly, no one wants to appear the fool or to feel swindled. Nor do people want to learn they have bought the wrong thing or have been persuaded to buy something they didn't need. If you stress how well suited your product is to the prospect's needs and how others who have bought it have benefited from it, you will find that the almost-universal desire for acceptance can increase your chances of making the sale.

Satisfying Motivations

Once you have identified both the needs and the buying motivations at work on a prospect, you are in a good position to satisfy the must-haves and to create the would-like-to-haves so essential to a sale. As you analyze your prospect's needs and desires, review in your mind the features and advantages of your product and the benefits they produce. In that way, you will be able to stress benefits that will satisfy the motivations of the prospect.

Begin here to think specifically about your prospects and customers. What motivates them to buy? Why? How do you know? For example, security may be a strong motive among homeowners considering your house-cleaning service. They are concerned that their valuables be safe from theft, their home free from burglary. They reveal this motive by their questions about your process of screening employees and your bonding procedures or by their comments about security and safety. As you give thought to your prospective customers, fill in Table 2.1.

TABLE 2.1.   BUYING MOTIVES AT WORK ON YOUR PROSPECTS

Buying motive	Yes/No	Why?	How does it appear?
Financial benefit			
Security			
Convenience			
Sex appeal			
Fear			
Pleasure			
Acceptance			

APPLYING PRODUCT KNOWLEDGE

One of the most common shortcomings many tellsellers have, one they share with salespeople everywhere, is that they sell product features and advantages instead of product benefits. As one sales philosopher put it, "You should not be selling a half-inch drill bit. You should be selling all the benefits of a half-inch hole."

Let's assume, for the moment, that you are working for USA National Life Insurance Company. What are you selling? "Why," you'd answer, "I'm selling life insurance policies."

Let's be a little more imaginative now and say you are selling "provision for a family's financial needs in the event of the prospect's untimely death." You have strengthened your selling statement by supporting the *feature*—insurance on a life—with an *advantage* of that feature of your company's product. If you stopped your presentation there, you probably would not make the sale. What you are really selling, and have not yet stated, is financial gain, security (peace of mind), and convenience. These are the *benefits* that lead a prospect to buy life insurance.

Features

A *feature* is a description of the product in terms of its real or perceived specifications. Features define what the product is, the characteristics that combine to make it unique. Some features of different products are shown in Figure 2.1 on page 28.

Select a product you will be selling on the telephone and write it here:

_____

Now, describe in two or three key phrases or sentences what the features of that product are:

1. _____

2. _____

3. _____

Advantages

Knowing the advantages that each product feature produces is of even greater interest to your prospect than is knowing the features. An *advantage* ex-

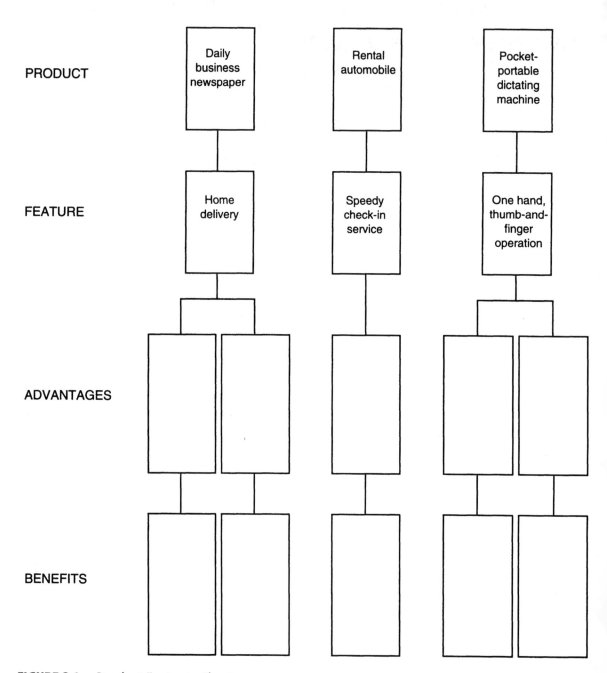

FIGURE 2.1. Product Features Chart

plains what a feature will do for the user. Each feature will have one or more advantages.

Returning to your role as a teleseller for USA National Life Insurance, what are the advantages to the prospect of this feature of your product: "guaranteed lifetime renewal protection" (the company cannot cancel the policy once issued)? At least two come to mind. First, coverage cannot be canceled for *any* reason. Also, because this feature makes physical condition irrelevant, the insured will not have to undergo periodic physical examinations to keep the policy in force.

Figure 2.2 on page 30 shows advantages of the features shown in Figure 2.1.

You will notice that every feature of the chart in Figure 2.2 has at least one advantage. You will find that very often features have several advantages.

Return to the list of product features you wrote on page 27 and write the second one you listed:

_____

Using phrases and sentences, write at least two advantages that the feature offers to those who would use your product. (Remember, an advantage is a description of what the feature—not the product—does for the user.)

1. _____

2. _____

3. _____

Benefits

The final, and key, element of product knowledge is learning the product's *benefit* to the user. Benefits are what the prospect or customer will gain from the advantages of your product. In order to close a sale, you will need to make a connection between your product's features and advantages and the prospect's needs and buying motivations. That connection is the product's benefits.

How, then, do prospects gain by having "guaranteed lifetime renewal protection"? Tying the benefit to buying motivations, you would stress that they no longer need to fear being canceled. And they are free from the resulting inconvenience of finding new insurance. Don't forget the convenience that comes from being able to handle their insurance needs from their home,

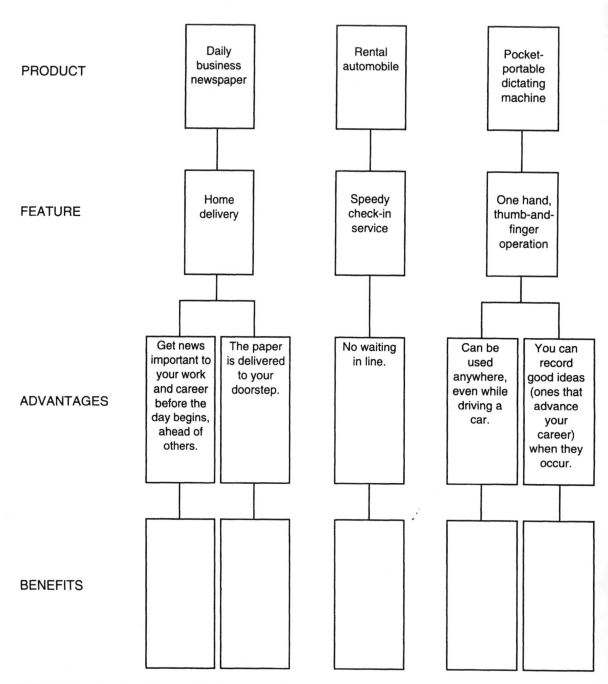

FIGURE 2.2. Product Features/Advantages Chart

by telephone. Finally, they won't ever have to worry about their family's financial security.

Figure 2.3 on page 32 lists several possible benefits of the other products presented. Look the chart over carefully before continuing. This will give you a feel for how advantages can be translated into benefits for all kinds of products.

Now, return to the advantages you listed on page 29. Select one and write it here:

_____

Identify the benefits the prospect will gain from this advantage. (Remember: The benefit is produced by the advantage, not by the product or its feature.)

1. _____

2. _____

3. _____

Prepare a blank chart like the one in Figure 2.1. Duplicate a sufficient quantity to be able to list the key features of each product you are going to sell. Begin by asking yourself which features are most important for the type of prospect you are going to be calling. Limit yourself, initially, to three to six features, and place them in the appropriate spaces. Go on to list the advantages that each feature has. Finally, list the benefits that those advantages are likely to have to the prospects you will be calling.

Each feature is likely to have more than one advantage, and several advantages can be combined to produce one benefit. In other words, benefits-selling is not a mathematical exercise. It is a mental process whereby you mix and match what you know about your product with what you learn as you listen to each prospect. Over time, you will find that your prospects also make their own contributions to your benefits list.

Making Effective Calls

Now, ask yourself just what you should get across in the calls you handle. Which features, advantages, and benefits are essential to understanding the gain to be had from your product? In the beginning, keep to the basics, usually as stressed by your product sales literature. As you talk to prospects and customers, be alert to what *they* think is important. It may make you rethink the things you wrote down.

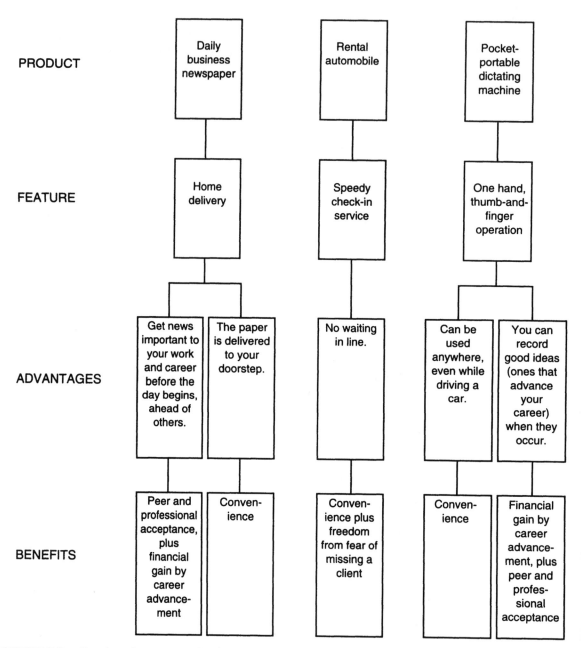

	Daily business newspaper	Rental automobile	Pocket-portable dictating machine
PRODUCT	Daily business newspaper	Rental automobile	Pocket-portable dictating machine
FEATURE	Home delivery	Speedy check-in service	One hand, thumb-and-finger operation
ADVANTAGES	Get news important to your work and career before the day begins, ahead of others. / The paper is delivered to your doorstep.	No waiting in line.	Can be used anywhere, even while driving a car. / You can record good ideas (ones that advance your career) when they occur.
BENEFITS	Peer and professional acceptance, plus financial gain by career advancement / Convenience	Convenience plus freedom from fear of missing a client	Convenience / Financial gain by career advancement, plus peer and professional acceptance

FIGURE 2.3. Product Features/Advantages/Benefits Chart

32

Of course, the most valuable aspect of your Features/Advantages/Benefits charts is the benefits boxes. Write out as many benefits statements as you can and begin committing them to memory. You will then have sales-closing information and a ready guide to benefits statements on the tip of your tongue during a sales call.

Follow that by applying your knowledge to simulated sales situations. If possible, role-play sales calls to test yourself from a customer's point of view. What will you say if a customer asks a certain question? How does your answer sound?

There are other immediate dividends that come from knowing your product well. Regardless of the sales success of the call you are making at the moment, you will build respect for your professionalism that can pay off in the future. If you are selling to a prospect base that requires you to make repeated contacts, whether to close the sale in the first place or to service buyers, you will be remembered as a sincere business person who has the customer's interests at heart. You will answer questions and objections more effectively. And, as your self-confidence grows, you will feel more and more comfortable making your calls.

You will see opportunities to sell in direct proportion to how much you know about your prospect's buying motives and the benefits of your product. The pieces of information you gain from many different sources will all combine in a synergistic manner to make you an increasingly effective teleseller. You will be more sincere and empathetic, will speak with more conviction, will handle calls more efficiently, and will close more sales.

ON YOUR OWN

1. Which of the seven buying motives outlined in this chapter (see pages 24–26) will your prospects be seeking to satisfy?

2. For each buying motive you listed answering question 1, identify the ways in which that buying motive is expressed in your industry. For example, for "financial gain," someone selling car insurance might note "My customers always look for ways to save money on their premium"; for "security," someone selling textbooks might indicate "Math instructors want to be sure there are no errors in the solutions section of their textbooks."

3. How do your products satisfy each buying motive that you have detailed in question 2? For example, a car-insurance teleseller might offer

savings on premiums by saying: "Our multivehicle discount saves twenty percent off the premium" or "If you increase your deductible for collision and comprehensive damage, you'll save an additional seventy-five dollars on your premium."

Remember, prospects are seeking to satisfy their buying motives. Your products deliver benefits to those who use them. The terms that describe buying motives and product benefits are identical. Use product benefits to satisfy each buying motive.

SELF-INVENTORY

	Yes	No
1. I provide my prospects and customers with a needed and valued product.	___	___
2. I know and understand what motivates people to buy the product I am selling.	___	___
3. I am thoroughly acquainted with my company's product and what it does.	___	___
4. I translate product features and the resulting advantages into benefits for prospects.	___	___
5. I have all relevant sales literature at hand to consult as needed while I am on the telephone with a prospect.	___	___

3 A Basic Sales-Call Strategy

THE KEY

There are very few secrets to success in teleselling. The formula for success is simple enough for anyone to understand: mastery of the skills necessary to conduct effective telephone sales interviews, multiplied by hard work. To begin to master the necessary teleselling skills, though, you do need to be let in on one secret, which you will learn in the first section of this chapter. Further, as you plan your calls, you must be aware of the aspects of your behavior as a teleseller that produce a positive reaction in the people you contact. Once you are aware of the one true secret of selling and know how people are going to react to you when you contact them, you can begin to plan your sales calls accordingly.

THE ONLY TRUE SECRET OF SELLING: THE CALL FLOW

Teleselling, because it is a human activity, is more art than science. It requires a combination of knowledge and skill, of intelligence and alertness, of attitude and empathy. Armed with these qualities, you can guide and direct telephone calls to a successful outcome: whether that is the making of an appointment, closing a sale, or providing customer service after the sale.

The first step in the process is to gain an understanding of what is going on in a sales call. Look at this example of shopping for clothes.

You have been invited to a reception sponsored by one of your suppliers. Excited at the prospect of meeting others in your industry, you want to look your best. You scan your closet and decide it is time to buy a new outfit for the occasion. You head off to the mall, money in hand, and aim right for your favorite clothing store (or you might, if you're like me, dig out your favorite clothing catalog and place your order by telephone). In the space provided or on a separate sheet of note paper, outline the steps that will occur in your shopping experience:

_____

_____

_____

_____

_____

_____

_____

_____

_____

_____

_____

_____

What steps did you include? Compare yours with the following six steps:

1. As you walked in, you were greeted by the salesperson saying something like, "Good afternoon. What can I help you with today?" Did you return this acknowledgment of your presence?

2. Depending on whether you asked the salesperson to assist you or preferred to shop undisturbed, you probably headed for the clothing item(s) you were after. If you were buying slacks to match a blazer, what color would you look for? What fabric? What size? What style? How much would you spend? Knowing that you wanted, say, tan cotton slacks, size medium, slim, with pleats, no cuffs, you no doubt looked through the selection available. How many choices did you find?

3. You took the pair(s) of slacks that would suit you to the dressing room to try on. How did they look? How did they fit and feel? Suppose the ones that fit you the best had just a little too much olive green in the tan. What would you do?

4. If you are like most shoppers, you headed back to the section where you found those slacks and picked up one or two other shades of tan to try on. As you tried each one on, you asked questions of the salesperson, whose help you had by now enlisted. Perhaps the salesperson went to another area of the store to get yet another pair of slacks, ones you had overlooked in your search.

5. Finally, after trying on several pairs of slacks, you found the perfect addition to your wardrobe.

6. The salesperson then either directed you to a cashier or wrote up the sale for you. What methods of payment were available—credit card, cash, check, gift certificate, a merchandise credit, or traveler's check? Did the salesperson suggest accessories—a belt, a shirt, socks? Was your merchandise put in a bag for you? Was the store's refund policy posted or stated? Did the purchase end with a "thank you" from the salesperson or cashier?

A flowchart of your experience might look like Figure 3.1 on page 38.

Assuming the overall experience was a pleasant one for you, how often would you repeat the six-step process described? Two or three times a day? Once a day? Once a week? Once a month? Once or twice a year? Odds are that shopping is a sometimes thing for you, an experience to which you look forward and one that gives you a good feeling, especially when you find just what you are looking for.

How many times a day do you think the salesperson who helped you goes through the same six-step experience with other shoppers? On average, a clothing store employee can expect to handle eight situations just like yours every hour. What for you is a relatively uncommon, often enjoyable event,

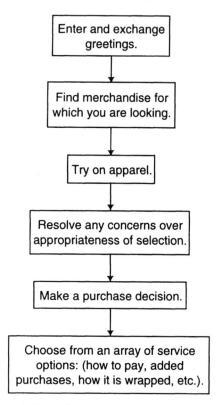

FIGURE 3.1. A Buyer's Experience

for the salesperson is an everyday, common phenomenon that seems to follow the same pattern virtually every time a sale is made.

That's the secret: *All sales calls, whether or not a sale is made, unfold in exactly the same order.* Whether you are deciding what to have for a snack during your work break or what telecommunications equipment to purchase to make your unit more cost-effective, the sales-call flow pattern will be virtually identical to the one you outlined for your purchase of slacks.

Knowing this, you are ready to plan for the buyer's experience. You can outline the event (we've already done that). You can give thought to what you will say at each step along the way. You can practice how you want to respond to what the prospective buyer says. You can anticipate the twists and turns inherent in applying a process—the sales-call strategy—to a wide variety of buyers. You can even guide buyers through the process when they are reluctant to follow.

HOW TO INFLUENCE YOUR PROSPECTIVE CUSTOMER

When you do go shopping and are approached by a salesperson, how do you react? Are you like most people and want to be left alone? If so, you no doubt respond to the greeting politely but rebuff the offer of help from the smiling, pleasant, attentive salesperson. You may, as many do, instantly adopt your "I'm in the presence of a salesperson" defenses: You curtly say, "No thanks, I'm just browsing," you refuse to make eye contact, and you hurry off to another area of the store.

Sales professionals know that people react differently to them in their selling role than they might if they met them in social circumstances. Knowing this, you want to determine what it is about you, the *salesperson,* that makes prospective buyers react as they do. And while each prospect is different and, for that reason, no two calls are the same, you can still generalize about how prospects react when you call. Such reactions not only determine how well you establish rapport, but ultimately whether or not you make or lose a sale.

Interest

Studies indicate that prospects are most influenced by their perception of a salesperson's *interest* in them as individuals and in their needs, wants, desires, concerns, and problems. This is true whether the prospects are individual consumers or business buyers. As much as one-half of a prospect's reaction to salespeople depends on this one perception. That is why this book places so much emphasis on your ability to analyze needs and to empathize and establish rapport.

How do you demonstrate your sincere interest in a prospect's needs, wants, desires, concerns, and problems? Consciously or unconsciously, a prospect will listen for several clues. What questions do you ask? Do you ask the questions in order to learn the prospect's wants and needs? Do the questions help the prospect make an intelligent buying decision? Do you listen while the prospect is talking? Are you open-minded in your approach, never doggedly trying to sell something before you determine the prospect's needs? Do you project an attitude of helpfulness throughout the call, demonstrating a desire to serve, not sell? If you do all of this, you establish that you have the interests of the prospect uppermost in your mind.

Credibility

A second important factor is your *credibility*. The accuracy of the information you give is critical if you are to prevent misunderstandings and build trust. This factor can count for as much as one-fourth of the prospect's evaluation of you and your call. Do you make either subtle or obvious errors in your presentation? Do you contradict yourself at any step of the contact? Are you careless or glib? Do you give deceptive or evasive answers to tough questions from the prospect? Any of these practices can cost you sales. You must be accurate in what you say to your prospects.

Because the credibility of the information you impart is almost as important as your interest in a prospect, you want to be sure that your information is not misunderstood and that the prospect doesn't feel misinformed, either of which can kill a sale. Information is judged by how accurate, complete, clear, and concise it is. Your product knowledge and basic selling and communication skills are important in projecting an image of truthfulness.

Speech

What kind of impression do your *speech habits* make? These include not only your enunciation and pronunciation, but also your choice of words, your pitch and tone of voice, and your rate of speech. Up to one-fifth of the contact's reaction is to your speech habits and mannerisms, so they are well worth paying attention to. Strong regional accents can be a problem, especially if you must talk to prospects in all parts of the country (you may even have to deal with regional prejudices). Your speech habits, if you are careless, can offend prospects.

Your speech itself is being evaluated. While not as important as your demonstrated interest or the credibility of your information, sloppy speech habits can put off a prospect. Remember, a failure to properly execute any of the mentioned points will result in your projecting a poor image of yourself.

Image

The fourth important factor is the *overall impression* you make. As much as one-tenth of the reaction you create is based on the image you project, even though you are selling on the telephone and not in the presence of the prospect. Sales professionals know that image counts, whether it is visible or not. Only you can determine if it will count for or against you.

In face-to-face situations, people judge others by their appearance—the image they create—based on such factors as how well their clothing is suited to the work they are doing, how they carry themselves, and how they are groomed. The importance of your image as a teleseller doesn't disappear just because you aren't visible. Think of how often you create a mental picture of a person you can hear but not see—a radio announcer, for example, or a person in another room. When you are talking on the telephone, you, too, are being visualized. The prospect is forming a mental image of what you look like on the basis of things you say and do.

How does a prospect create an image of you? Many individual things add up to present a composite picture of you. Some of these are obvious: voice, vocabulary, rate of speech, grammar, enunciation, any regional dialect you may have. Then there are subtler suggestions of your appearance: how professionally you answer the call or introduce yourself, how well you conduct the interview, and what background sounds can be heard while you talk.

What about your vocal mannerisms: Do you show that you are paying attention? Do you use slang or industry jargon? Are you sarcastic? Do you inject controversial subjects into the conversation? Do you make outlandish statements?

It is a good idea to ask yourself right now, "What kind of image am I projecting? How do I appear over the telephone?" Remember, as much as one-fifth of your possible success is riding on the impression you make, even on the telephone.

Draw up a list of at least five characteristics you exhibit as you "appear" on the telephone.

1. _____

2. _____

3. _____

4. _____

5. _____

Courtesy

The final element in the prospect's reaction, accounting for perhaps another one-tenth of the total, will hinge on *courtesy*: your being appropriately polite in your dealings with your prospect. The key word here is *appropriately*. Your work requires nothing more than normal good manners. Excesses in either direction—on the one hand, abrupt, short, abrasive remarks and a condescending attitude, or, on the other hand, downright servility—will get you in trouble and will cost you sales.

The telephone imposes some limitations and creates a few unique opportunities to demonstrate courtesy. There are things you can do to conduct yourself in a courteous manner. List the things you presently do or can do to project a polite image over the telephone:

1. _____

2. _____

3. _____

4. _____

5. _____

The first step in true courtesy is putting yourself in your prospect's place (empathizing). Your attitude should reflect your willingness to be of service in all of your dealings with her or him. More specifically, your list could include:

- Answering the telephone promptly if you are handling incoming calls (recommended policy is to answer on the third ring if possible).

- Identifying yourself and your company right away.

- Personalizing the call by using the prospect's name at every *reasonable* opportunity, without overdoing it (remember, you are not a friend; keep it polite but formal, using the person's last name, not a first name).

- Expressing your willingness to be of service (for example, saying, "Yes, Mr. Wolfe, how may I help you?").

- Being easy to talk to and deal with.

- Showing your appreciation with such simple but often overlooked phrases as "thank you" or "I appreciate that."

- Telling a person how long you will be when you put them on hold (saying "I'll just be a second" and then coming back on the line after several minutes can irritate people).

- Hanging up after the prospect does, if this is possible without being awkward.

One precaution: Moderation is the best policy. Elaborate politeness is likely to put off the prospect. Be naturally courteous, and you will get the favorable reaction you want.

These, then, are the factors that determine how prospects or customers react to you when you make contact with them. They evaluate you on the basis of:

- The interest you show in their problems and needs

- The credibility of the information you dispense

- Your speech

- The image you create for yourself

- Your manners

Throughout this book we will come back to these elements. For now, memorize them. They are the backbone of the system of selling that you should make a part of your unconscious work habits.

Finally, you must consider how many times and over what period of time you will be in touch with a prospect. This will influence how much importance to place on the various aspects of the call and will determine how much time you have to work on ensuring that you will be received positively.

To be successful at selling you should use a selling system that does two critical things for you:

1. Takes the call through the necessary steps of the call flow.

2. Enables the prospect to react favorably to you.

A basic and simple call strategy that applies to all situations and contexts and that can become part of your unconscious behavior will get the response you want.

CALL STRATEGY AND THE PURPOSE OF THE CALL

Each sales interview provides an opportunity to close a sale. As the teleseller, it is up to you to guide the course of the call to that end. In order to move from the rapport you begin to establish with your initial "hello" to the close of a sale before you say "good-bye," you will need to follow a call strategy that will serve you in every call you handle.

What are your goals—what do you want to accomplish in your calls? Are you "cold calling" the target market looking for prospects? Qualifying these prospects? Closing sales? Making appointments? Servicing customers? Or are you doing follow-up selling to your regular buyers?

Once you have established your goals, you will employ a time-tested, systematic, and logical method of controlling the sales interview. The system naturally leads the prospect through a planned, step-by-step conversation, minimizing objections. This strategy can work for you whether you are making a one-call close or a multicall sale.

The strategy consists of six steps—the straight A's of teleselling: approach, analyze, advocate, answer, ask, and apply.

1. *Approach the prospect and gain his or her attention by using an opening remark that stresses benefits.*   The first two buying decisions a prospect has to make are (1) whether to talk with you in the first place—this is decided when the prospect picks up the telephone—and (2) whether to continue to listen to what you have to say. An attention-grabbing approach is designed to get your prospect interested in listening to you further. In teleselling, it is estimated that you have about twenty seconds for this vital step because, unless you have made an appointment in advance, you are probably interrupting the person you are calling. You must get a lot of impact into what you say immediately after introducing yourself. So the importance of your attention-grabber cannot be overstated.

2. *Analyze the prospect's needs and build interest through questioning.*   Effective selling requires that you know your prospect's needs so you can show him that what you offer will satisfy those needs. Through questioning and listening, you also build interest and start to create a desire or need to buy. If you are planning to work from a script (see Chapter 15), you will have to give a lot of forethought to your prospect's likely needs and will have to work them into the prepared presentation in advance.

3. *Advocate the appropriate product(s) to create a desire or need to buy.* You make a product recommendation and emphasize the product's benefits that will satisfy the needs your analysis has uncovered. Only when prospects see what's in it for them will they make a favorable buying decision.

4. *Answer questions and objections persuasively.* Unless you are the sole source of something everyone needs for survival, people are going to raise questions about, even object to, buying what you are selling. You must answer these questions and objections in your selling strategy. Here, you are again persuading the prospect to buy, removing any obstacles that may exist.

5. *Ask for the order as a natural conclusion to your call.* If you have effectively followed the first four steps, asking for an order will get you the sales action that motivated your call. The prospect becomes a customer.

6. *Apply appropriate follow-up service to make and keep a satisfied customer.* After the sale is made, you will cement a lasting favorable relationship by taking pains to ensure smooth order fulfillment and user satisfaction. Applying service at all points of prospect and customer contact will keep your hard-won customers among your active accounts.

The flow of a typical sales call is illustrated in Figure 3.2 on page 46. You can see that it is not as rote and orderly a process as the description of it would suggest. How closely your calls will follow this pattern will be determined by a variety of factors, including your use of the six-step strategy, your call goal and strategy, and the behavior of your prospects. However, if you compare Figure 3.2 with Figure 3.1, you can see that the steps recommended as a call flow exactly parallel the steps in a shopper's decision-making process.

Your call strategy has to be easy to remember so that you can begin to use it immediately. (Note that each step's label begins with an **A** as a memory aid for you.) With repetition it will become natural, automatic behavior. You won't have to consciously think about it; you will be able to concentrate on using the selling skills you have acquired. You will be able to respond to each call naturally, confidently, and successfully. Then you will close more and more of your calls with a sale.

ON YOUR OWN

1. What marketing activity are you going to undertake on the telephone?

2. What is your objective in this activity?

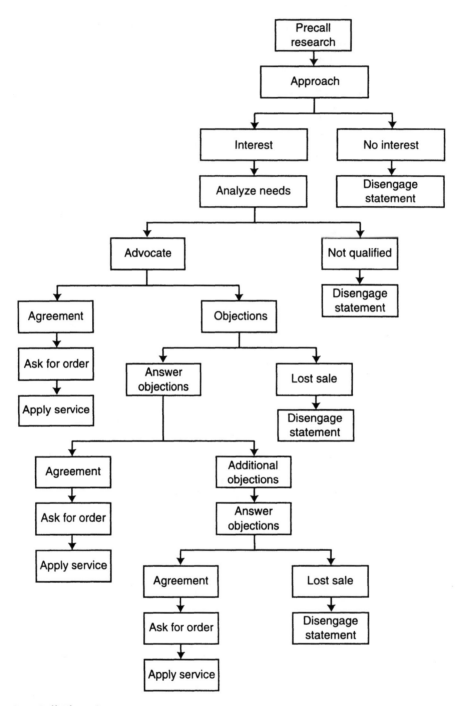

FIGURE 3.2. Call-Flow Pattern

46

3. What role does each step of the six-step strategy—approach; analyze needs; advocate a product; answer questions and objections; ask for the order; apply a service attitude—play in helping you achieve your goal?

		Yes	No
SELF-INVENTORY	1. My call objective is clear in my mind before I pick up the telephone.	____	____
	2. I recognize the need to guide and direct each call to the conclusion I desire.	____	____
	3. I know the mechanics of sales contact and apply them to the selling and buying process in my business.	____	____
	4. I use a logical sales plan to help me get to my call objectives.	____	____
	5. I am prepared to make a sale in each situation I encounter.	____	____

4 Prospecting

THE KEY

The purpose of prospecting is to reduce the world at large to a list of those most likely to buy from you immediately or in the near future—and to do it quickly and efficiently. While much of this activity goes on before you make your telephone call, prospecting begins in earnest once you get someone you suspect is a prospect on the line. When done correctly, prospecting allows you to spend a majority of your selling time where it will do the most good: talking to those who have a current need for your product. As you read this chapter, concentrate on how the techniques presented apply specifically to you. Once you have learned how to identify decision makers and get through to them when you call, you can set up record-keeping procedures to begin measuring your results.

KNOWING WHOM TO CALL

So there you sit by the telephone. You know your products well enough to talk knowledgeably about them with others. You have a call strategy in mind that will enable you to close sales. You are ready. But whom, among the more than 250 million people in the country, are you going to talk with?

For most salespeople, prospecting is probably the hardest part of selling. You begin work excited about your product and wanting to sell it. All your product knowledge leads you to think of it as the best product available. The people you call should need only to be told about it to buy it.

The Numbers

You begin to make your calls, and you suddenly learn that not everyone who should be interested in your product will even talk with you, let alone buy what you are selling. Some are downright rude to you. As you make your way from the more than 250 million individuals in the United States to the ones among them who will buy from you, you will encounter a lot of rejection—most of it in the prospecting phase.

The numbers involved show how difficult prospecting is. If you were to start from scratch, you would have to contact fifty people to produce one *suspect*: a person who (1) should have a need for your product, (2) has the available financial resources to buy your product, and (3) has access to your channel of distribution. Then, for every three suspects you uncover, one will be a *prospect*: someone you know can benefit from your product. From every three prospects, one will emerge as a *qualified* prospect: a person in the market for your product at the time of your contact. And, from three qualified prospects, you will close one sale. As you can see from Table 4.1, when you merely make cold calls to a list of households or businesses, you are faced with contacting approximately 450 people to close one sale. The need for you to learn to prospect effectively is obvious—a success rate of only 0.2 percent is not very satisfying, nor is it compelling (one sale in every 450 calls does not pay well).

Narrowing the Universe

Remember that the main objective of prospecting is to produce as large a list as possible of names and telephone numbers of "human beings who have been carefully selected for contact based on characteristics that indicate close affinity with our products and services." The first step in this process is to narrow a large undifferentiated universe—parents of children

TABLE 4.1. PROSPECTING AS A NUMBERS GAME

Selling activity		Number of calls		
Cold calls to produce a suspect	1	50	150	450
Suspects to produce a prospect		1	3	9
Qualified prospects to close			1	3
Closes				1

under five years of age, or all retail clothing outlets, or homeowners in the city of Cincinnati—down to suspects. You will find help in the form of mailing lists, subscriber lists, and so on.

Mailing lists are available from firms that specialize in compiling or managing them. Especially valuable as a source of such firms is the Standard Rate & Data Service's publication *Direct Marketing List Source.*

Another source of suspect names is special-interest-publication subscriber lists. In Ulrich's annual *International Periodicals Directory*, published by R. R. Bowker, you can find, for example, a total of ninety-nine publications addressed to *key* people in the grocery trades. Specialty markets can be accessed through such publications as *Beverage Aisle*, with 20,000 subscribers, or *Convenience Store News*, with 118,000 subscribers. If your market is limited geographically to, say, the South, you might find prospects among subscribers to *Alabama-Mississippi Grocers' Digest* (800 subscribers), *Arkansas Grocer* (3,000), and *Florida Grocer* (16,000). You can contact the circulation department of any publication in whose subscriber list you are interested. The circulation manager will tell you if the list is available, from whom (if not from them), and if it can include telephone numbers. Do check the reputation of any list vendors or publications whose lists you are contemplating using—and, in the case of vendors, where the lists you are getting come from. Ask for and consult references. How successful was the list for the referenced users? Was its use close enough to your intentions to give you any insight into how it will do for you? You might have to pay a slight extra charge for telephone numbers, or you could use one of the available telephone-number look-up services.

If you are selling to businesses, one useful tool might be the Standard Industrial Classification (SIC) number. This is a categorization of businesses according to primary activity. Almost every industry has one, including even nudist camps (#7032) and ping-pong parlors (#7999). Learn the SIC numbers of your target audiences so that you can more readily identify them when looking for mailing lists or studying the demographics provided by such agencies as your state's department of labor and industry or your local chamber of commerce. You can find a list of all SIC numbers in *The Standard Industrial Classification Manual*, available from the U.S. Government Printing Office, Washington, D.C. 20402.

Finally, don't rule out the use of the telephone to help you qualify suspects. You might be interested, for example, in selling to eyeglass-frame manufacturers who offer a line of children's frames. But the only list available is for all eyeglass-frame manufacturers. A teleblitz of such a list, with two or three key questions, can result in a list of known prospects in a short time. The telephone is ideal for such work: faster and more accurate than the mail and more cost-effective than conducting in-person interviews.

Identifying Prospects

Through responses to or follow-up on mailing campaigns, advertising, or a teleblitz campaign, you have identified most of those among the suspects who are legitimate prospects, people who should have an immediate need or desire for a product like yours. You probably identified them because of their behavior—they:

- Have bought similar items in the past.

- Are involved in some activity that indicates they may buy.

- Have responded to your (or a competitor's) advertising and promotion.

- Resemble, in their circumstances, others who have bought your products.

Again, mailing lists are a good source of prospects who have some or all of these characteristics. You may find lists broken down into the numerous applicable categories:

- *Individuals or businesses that have bought products like yours in the past.* Such lists are appropriate if the product is expendable, needs to be re-supplied, is such that owning one does not preclude owning others, or is suitable for replacement.

- *Individuals or businesses involved in specific activities that you know make them likely buyers of your product.* Members of health spas or country clubs might be in the market for sporting goods or might be wealthy enough to want your high-fashion magazine. Newly incorporated small businesses need office supplies or services. Sales managers with even the largest corporations might be able to use your product as a premium or your service as a means of reducing their cost of sales.

- *Individuals or businesses that have responded to an advertisement.* Anyone who has ordered a new subscription to a home-improvement magazine is a likely prospect for a variety of products, from tool sets to how-to books. A company that just requested free information on how to do presentations might be in the market for your business-communication consulting service or your audio-visual merchandise.

- *Individuals or businesses who resemble your known customers.* If your sales-tracking software for bank-platform personnel sells best to smaller regional banks with at least five branches, you would be advised to look for a list of managers of such banks in your market area who are not already your customers.

Do you keep in touch with existing customers, servicing their needs, recommending new applications for your product, and upgrading sales to newer or better products? It would be a serious mistake to take such people for granted. Your competition doesn't.

You should also keep names of former customers in a diary for appropriate regular contact. You might be able to sell them new benefits that arise from improvements in your product (or from additions to your product knowledge). If you don't keep in touch, you will never know when they grow dissatisfied with your competitor. Remember: The most likely source of new sales is your own customers, both current and former.

The checklist shown in Table 4.2 will help you begin to identify your own sources of suspects. Consider each source, note if it has any value to you (by "yes," "no," or some more elaborate annotation such as "much," "some," or "little"), and think about how you will go about tapping that source. Then draw up a plan to get suspects from each applicable source.

You have come a long way in a short period of time. You have moved from a pool of over 250 million people to a point where you are ready to place a call, make a sales presentation, and ask for an order, all with a reasonable chance for success.

TABLE 4.2. SOURCES OF SUSPECTS: A CHECKLIST

Sources	Value	Plan/Comments
Customer file		
Inactive accounts file		
Mailing lists		
SIC directories		
Telephone directories		
Cold calling		

PRECALL RESEARCH

In selling to businesses, especially with more complex products or in a situation that requires more than one or two calls, your prospecting may include some degree of initial and ongoing research and data gathering. This precall research is to acquaint you as thoroughly as possible with the prospect company, the person (or persons) involved in the buying decision, and the buying process.

Call Goals

The extent of this research depends on the context of the call in your marketing plan and your call goals. Is this a service call? Or are you trying:

- To develop leads?

- To draw attention to your company or product?

- To pave the way for an in-person visit?

- To refine your analysis of needs so you can more persuasively present the right product from your line?

- To put the finishing touches on a live product presentation?

- To close a sale on which you have been working?

Knowing the marketing context of your telephone call and what you want to accomplish tells you what you have to learn about the prospect or his or her company before you call.

Selling to individuals.   What kind of information do you need? A consumer's income level? Marital status? Whether the prospect is a home owner? Age? Occupation? Number of children and/or pets? Recent major purchase? The list may seem endless. Control it by concentrating on what really matters.

Selling to businesses.   What do you need to know about a company before you call? Its size, whether as revealed by assets, sales volume, or number of employees? What kind of business it is in? What types of equipment it uses? How it markets what it makes? If its credit rating is acceptable?

How does a company produce or service its product? Is it mass produced, produced on a cycle (like clothing), or produced on demand? Is it experiencing increased or diminishing demand? Where does the product you are selling fit in? Make a list of the information you need, item by item.

Information Sources

Where can you find the information needed? There are several possible sources: You may already have helpful *files* at your work station to get you started. *Records* may exist within your own company that will give you information. It may be helpful for you to talk with some of your *known contacts* at the prospect's place of business or to similar people from among your customers. The *business section* of your local library may contain useful sources of information. Your own *past experiences* with others like the prospect or the company you are attempting to sell may help.

Add these sources to ones you might already know about, perhaps ones available only in your industry or markets, and you have a good data base to turn to when you want to research your prospects before calling them.

PROSPECTING STRATEGIES

Calling Plan

Make a card file with the names of the individual consumers or the names of companies and the contact person you intend to call. When each card has all necessary information, get on the telephone and begin selling. Plan to make the maximum use of calling time. Develop a work plan to make good use of your time on the telephone by doing all your preparation and follow-up during noncalling hours.

At the end of the day or before your first call in the morning, review your prospect cards. Plan to call a sufficient number of prospects to make a full day's work. Figure on ten calls an hour to businesses, twenty calls an hour to individuals or for other teleblitz campaigns. Of course, as you gain experience, adjust the hourly goal. The ten or twenty calls per hour recommended here is based on experience in a variety of markets. Resist the temptation to lower the goal.

Have your prospect cards in whatever order you find appropriate: alphabetically, by industry, by location, or by some particular attribute. Then work your way through the cards in the order that your plan dictates. Don't be tempted to jump around just because some of the calls don't work out to your satisfaction. The old adage "Plan your work and work your plan" applies here, as it does most places in selling. If you fall into the bad habit of dropping your plan and then eventually not making a plan, you won't survive the long run. Refer back to Table 4.1. How many calls do you have to make to close a sale or reach your other goals? How many sales do you have to make to reach your quota? How much extra can you make by exceeding your quota? How long will it take you to do that?

Calling Problems

With your first telephone call, you are likely to encounter two substantial problems that deserve special attention and preparation on your part: *first*, almost exclusively the concern of business teleselling, *getting through the call screens* set up within companies; *second*, characteristic of both individual and business teleselling, *determining who has the authority to buy*.

Getting through to the person you want to talk with is known as *penetrating the screen*. The screen is typically composed of a switchboard operator and the decision maker's secretary. Experienced tellsellers will tell you that trying to penetrate a screen is their most frustrating task.

But there are general procedures to help you penetrate screens. They vary with your goals, your market, and your personality, and those of your prospect. It will be appropriate to behave one way if you are making a one-call close with no likely follow-up contact regardless of the outcome of the call, and another way if you are trying to establish a long-term selling relationship with your contact. In addition, you must give thought to the behavior with which you are comfortable. The four techniques described here will not work for all people in all situations, but one of them will work for you in your situation.

Get around the screen.   Your attitude and behavior reflect your conviction that no one can stop you. You assume your best "voice of authority." Keep the screeners off balance by closing your answer to every question they pose with a counter-question. All this is aimed at convincing them of the urgency of your talking with the prospect or at intimidating them into putting you through.

Suppose you are asked, "What is this in reference to?" (1) You can be vague, even deceptive, and still be successful. Don't forget to end your answer with the question, "Is she in?" You should expect this method to alienate those on whom it is used. But if your call is a one-call close with no follow-up, you might decide that the prize in this case is worth the price. Or (2) you might answer the question with one of your best benefit statements, phrased in such a way as to make it seem as though the screener would be remiss if you were not put through. For example, if you got the decision maker's name from a list of known buyers of a related product, you might say, "He expressed interest in our technique for increasing levels of productivity. Is he in?"

Go below the screen.   Screeners tend to be 9-to-5 employees. They are also more likely to go out for lunch or to take a break at regularly scheduled times. To go below this person, call at a time when the screen isn't likely to be in place. Many executives and other decision makers come to work early, skip lunch for something at their desk while they get some more work done, and stay late to finish up the day's work. So, when you place your first call to a prospect and get a switchboard operator, ask immediately for the prospect's direct-dial or extension number. Note and use that number when calling at off times. You'll be pleasantly surprised when, at 7:30 A.M. (or 5:30 P.M.), your decision maker, the one the screener would not let you through to, picks up the telephone.

Going above the screen.   Going above the screen might require more extensive precall research and necessitate a more elaborate precall marketing strategy. But the technique is very effective in large organizations and can serve you well in medium and small businesses as well. Through research, identify the highest ranking officer in the company who is likely to benefit from buying your product. Call or write that person, presenting introductory information stressing benefits. Inform the executive that you will be calling to discuss this important subject in greater detail in a few days. Begin your teleselling account penetration with the promised call or with a cold call. You know you are likely to be referred to a lower level of the company, and you are ready. Calling the senior vice president of finance, you fully expect to be told to call the information systems manager to talk about your new money- and time-saving products. Now you are in a position to call the information systems manager and tell the ever-present secretary, the ultimate screener, that you were talking with the vice president of finance (or use her name), and she told you to speak with Ms. Jackson before getting back to her.

If you use this strategy, be on your guard that you don't get bounced too low in the decision ladder. You want to know, in advance if possible, who really makes buying decisions. If he relies on suggestions from other decision makers, you must involve all the concerned parties in the process. Again, the telephone facilitates your doing this with both calls and follow-up correspondence. Avoid being put in the situation where you have persuaded a non-decision maker to buy to the product. Then you are in the very unsatisfactory position of having a subordinate in a prospect or customer company trying to do your job for you—sell your product. You are the expert. The other person cannot sell as effectively as you can and might not even know how to sell. She almost certainly won't go out on a limb with the employer in order to close your sale. It is very tempting to talk with anyone who will listen, but know where to draw the line and don't go below the decision maker.

Work through the screen.   This technique is especially effective with those prospects to whom you will have to make many calls. It involves establishing a rapport with the screener.

1. Learn the person's name and use it.

2. Involve the screener in your process. Begin doing this in your introductory call or letter. End the announcement of your forthcoming call with a statement like, "Next week I will call your secretary to arrange an appointment for ten minutes of your uninterrupted time on the telephone."

3. Finally, be sincerely cooperative in your dealings with the screener in all the calls you make to close the sale and service the account.

A related technique, again working through the screen, is to build a sense of urgency and need about the purpose of the call. But don't tip your hand to the extent that the screener makes the buying decision for the decision maker. The best technique here is to write out one or two of your earlier benefits statements in a way that makes it a *benefit to the screener* to put you through to the decision maker. Try them, revise them, and try them again. Keep the ones your experience show work, and revise or scrap the ones that don't.

Experience has shown that involving the person who screens the decision maker's calls is the most effective technique in the long run. Your further reward will be those situations in which the screener cooperates with you, giving you valuable inside information that actually helps you sell to the company.

Identifying decision makers.   The other frequent problem you encounter, that of *identifying the decision maker in a buying situation*, can be just as frustrating as encountering the screen. It is important for you to know who is in a position to make the final buying decision. You don't want to make a full presentation, in one or several calls, only to learn that someone other than the person with whom you have been speaking will have to be persuaded before the purchase can be made. You should have been speaking with that other person in the first place. If you succeed in persuading the wrong person to order your product, it can result in increased costs and inconvenience to you and others in your company. You can be virtually certain the product will be returned or the order canceled once the real decision maker learns of the sale. You have lost not only money, but a lot of good will as well.

Business decisions.   Identifying the decision maker in a business can be a complex process. It may well be more than one person, requiring you to work vertically in a hierarchy, or horizontally among a committee of peers whose departments are affected by the buying decision. But often the best way to find out is simply to ask a direct question: "Do you make that decision, Mr. Johnson? Alone or with the concurrence of others?"

If you determine that the decision-making process is complex, or if you are having difficulty getting a clear picture of the situation, review these points and apply them to your situation:

1. While processes and key individuals can vary from industry to industry, within the same industry the processes are likely to be the same or similar. Refer to your experience with similar companies to guide you.

2. By starting as high in a hierarchy as possible, if you are bounced to a lower level, you have opened the door with the higher authority for follow-up.

3. The records in your company's files may help. Especially if your prospect is a former customer or if you are trying to increase sales to an existing customer, previous records may give you the insight you need.

4. It may be helpful to talk with other tellers who have experience with prospects like yours.

5. Job titles can be a good indicator of the authority hierarchy in a company. What do the titles of the parties involved tell you?

Individual consumer decisions.   If you are selling to individual consumers, again, your best strategy is to ask direct questions: "Mrs. Morris, is this a purchase you decide on? Do you consult any other member of the household?" Use the latter question *only* if you sense it is absolutely necessary.

You don't want to start Mrs. Morris thinking, "I'd better check with John before I say yes," and possibly kill a sale.

Whatever product you are selling, and regardless of the market, identifying the decision maker is always necessary and sometimes difficult. Be prepared to dig a little for the information you need. It will pay off in increased sales.

Productivity

You can evaluate your productivity by using the Weekly Progress Report in Table 4.3, which will help you distinguish among calls completed, screens encountered, decision makers reached, and presentations made to decision makers. In this way you can determine a pattern of likely success to be expected at each level. Remember, industry-wide experience shows you will be successful at penetrating the screener in one out of three cases. If you aren't doing that well, reconsider both the strategy you chose and what you are saying. Don't get discouraged. Just improve on what you do and say. And keep calling.

TABLE 4.3.   WEEKLY PROGRESS REPORT

Name: _____   Week of: _____

Day	Total calls	Contacts with decision makers	Presentations completed	Total prospects	Prospects ranked A	B	C	Referrals received*
Monday								
Tuesday								
Wednesday								
Thursday								
Friday								
Totals								

*Another potential source of prospects is your customers. If you have just closed a sale, completed a presentation that went well without resulting in an order, or finished servicing a customer, ask the other party for referrals to others who may be interested in your products. A textbook teleseller could ask, "Professor Huxtable, who else in the Anthropology Department teaches Cultural Anthropology? Would they consider using our text, with its strong emphasis on the biological bases of behavior?" The representative of a photography studio could ask, "Mrs. Miller, would others in your neighborhood [or family] benefit from our special offer?" Prepare a request-for-referrals statement to include in your sales call wrap-up strategy, and use it. Keep track of the number of referrals that result.

ON YOUR OWN

1. Go to the telephone directory for your community. If you are planning to sell to individual consumers, use the white pages and go on to 2. If you are planning to sell to businesses, use the yellow pages and go on to 3.

2. *If you are selling to individual consumers*: Beginning on the first page where names and numbers are listed, work your way down the page. Scan each entry and place a check beside each person you can call (eliminate such things as entries for more than one family member, the business numbers you encounter, and the like) until you have a total of sixty individuals with home telephone numbers. Now write out no more than three questions you will have to ask each of these individuals in order to determine whether or not they are qualified as a prospective buyer of your product(s).

3. *If you are selling to businesses*: Think of as many entry categories as possible where you would find businesses who are prospective buyers for your products. Turn to each category and, from the companies listed there, create a list of thirty company names and telephone numbers. Now think of the position title (Sales Manager, Maintenance Supervisor, or the like) for which you will ask when you call each company on your list. Write out no more than three questions you will have to ask each of these people in order to determine whether or not they are qualified as a prospective buyer of your product(s).

		Yes	No
SELF-INVENTORY	1. I take the time to do needed research before calling a prospect.	____	____
	2. I use the knowledge my research provides to establish rapport with the prospect.	____	____
	3. I know the person, by name and/or title, with whom I should talk before placing the call.	____	____
	4. I make sure I am talking to the person with the authority to buy before continuing the contact.	____	____
	5. My efforts to get through to decision makers are usually successful.	____	____

SPECIAL ACTIVITY: GETTING ON THE TELEPHONE

It's time to get on the telephone and sell. When you completed Table 1.2 on page 15, what did you decide about where and how you want to use the telephone? Whom can you call to start getting that done? Don't stall! Take your prospect list and start calling. Work from 9 A.M. to 5 P.M., in two three-hour shifts with only an occasional break.

Using the worksheet in Table 4.3, keep a record of how many calls you make in a day—approximately 60 business calls or 120 individual calls should be your goal. Also note how many decision makers you reach, how many actual sales interviews or presentations you make, if you close any sales, and what problems you encounter.

Remember: No matter how you do on your first day on the job, the sun will rise tomorrow, your family and friends still love you, and there will be more prospects for you tomorrow than there are today.

More important to your goals, once you have spent the six hours on the phone, you are ready to read and learn *effectively* from this book. Even if you are successful on the telephone today, you can always be *more* successful.

5 Approach

THE KEY

When you approach a prospect, you have the first twenty seconds of the call in which to secure her undivided attention. In order to be able to proceed beyond that time and achieve your call goal, you want to say something in that critical one-third of a minute that persuades your prospect that it is in her interest to talk with you. To best accomplish this, you should, after introducing yourself and your company, launch your conversation with an attention-grabbing approach statement that stresses one of your product's user benefits. This chapter discusses why an attention-grabber is necessary and shows you how to create ones that will work for you.

WHY GRAB THE PROSPECT'S ATTENTION?

The first challenge you face after getting your prospect on the telephone is to secure his attention for the duration of your call. While all salespeople face this challenge, it takes on increased importance in teleselling because your call may not have been expected and because it is coming from a remote location, which makes it easier to cut you off.

The prospect will decide whether he wants to listen to you further as a result of the first thirty words you say. What you say, then, must be carefully thought out in advance.

Your task is further complicated by the fact that the prospect is likely to be occupied with something completely unrelated to your call when it comes through. Whether you are calling an individual consumer or a business person, your call creates the need for the prospect to shift gears mentally; your attention-grabber facilitates that process.

Consider the advice, "First impressions count." Although prospects begin forming their impression of you the moment you say hello, the major impression begins forming as you start your introduction. What image do you want to create? How can you phrase and deliver an opening statement that fosters that image?

As teleselling catches on with a growing number of marketing organizations, there is also the increasing probability that you are not the only teleseller to call the prospect on that day. What can you say that will set you apart from the others in the prospect's mind? How can you overcome the possible irritation a prospect feels as his work is interrupted once more by a teleseller? A strong, no-nonsense, attention-grabbing opening statement can go a long way toward marking you as a professional worth listening to.

Finally, you need to persuade the prospect to want to listen further to what you have to say. So among its other tasks, your attention-grabber will also have to sell for the time you need to carry out your full strategy. A good opening will result in your having your prospect's undivided attention and will also stimulate an increased interest in your product. It might result not only in the realization of a need, but in the beginning of a desire to buy as well. And a strong, benefits-stressing opener can demonstrate your interest in your prospect and set the tone for the believability of the information you will be presenting.

You can achieve all of these effects with a preplanned, dramatic, interest-creating opening remark. If you employ a script for your entire sales interview, this will just be the first of several planned and memorized sections of your call. Avoid ad libbing or "winging it." Even if you plan to use an extemporaneous delivery for the bulk of your call, your opener should be planned—write it out, rehearse it, and deliver it verbatim. In fact, you should work to develop several different opening remarks that start your sales calls in a smooth, professional manner. As you use and improve on them, others will come to mind. In the end, you want to have as many different ways to open your call as needed to get and hold the attention of the many and varied prospects you encounter. And remember: Getting your prospect's attention turned exclusively to you is part of your effort to guide and direct the sales interview that begins the moment you say hello.

By planning your attention-grabbers carefully, and including a major prospect benefit in each one, you will get your calls off to a good start. When you have delivered an opening successfully, the prospect gives you close attention and wants to hear what else you have to say.

GETTING A PROSPECT'S UNDIVIDED ATTENTION

With the appropriate opening statements, you will grab a prospect's attention, and you are off to a good start in building a call that will conclude with a sale.

Attention-grabbing opening comments fall into several categories:

1. *A general statement that sparks interest*: You might say, "Mr. Wallace, I'm calling to make you aware of how companies like yours have saved up to 50 percent of their meeting budget by making intelligent use of our teleconferencing network." Or, "Market Aids' slide charts are attractive, useful giveaways that have increased paid orders as much as 40 percent. I'm calling, Mrs. Jacobi, to ask what your sales volume would be with a similar increase." Develop several interest-creating general comments, being sure that you are comfortable with them and that they reflect your personality and style.

2. *A sincere compliment*: You could begin with, "We at Jet-Away are as proud of the durability of our jet spray nozzles as you are of your company's on-time delivery record. And our users report cutting down the amount of time their trucks are out of service for cleaning. I'm sure you want to achieve the same cost savings." Or, in acting on a referral, you might begin by acknowledging praise volunteered by the prospect: "Thank you for passing on the nice things people at Ace Electronics had to say about us. I'm certain we can come up with a design that produces similar results for your company." The key word in this type of attention-grabber is *sincere*. If you employ elaborate or false sincerity, you could offend your prospects, give the appearance of talking down to them, or otherwise damage the accuracy of your other selling statements.

3. *Key questions to gain your prospect's attention*: An automobile insurance teleseller, making an outbound call to a mailed-in request for a premium quote, might see from the request that the prospect only has $5,000 in property damage coverage. She should begin the call by asking, "From the information you provided, I wondered what provisions you have made in the event you strike another car and it is a total loss" and then point out, "At today's prices, 83 percent of all cars on the road are valued in excess of your $5,000 coverage." A textbook teleseller might ask a prospective user, "I called to ask what you are going to do next semester now that the book you are using in class is out of print."

4. *A startling statement that forces people to sit up and take notice*: This technique is more difficult but equally effective. Those selling homeowner's insurance policies often employ statements like, "Mr. Wynne, eight out of every ten people don't have enough coverage to replace their homes at present costs. If you are one of those eight, we can give you that protection, automatically, perhaps even at a lower premium than you are paying now."

5. *An analogy that captures your listener's interest*: From experience, you know that your prospect faces problems similar to those of others with whom you have dealt. Relate those problems and your solutions directly to the prospect. You might say, "Mrs. Hipple, our customized exterminating service helped the Winkler Bakery in Jefferson City eliminate rodents in their storage area in under three days, using techniques that protected the safety of the company's ingredients." After a pause, ask, "What do you do to combat vermin in your bakery?"

The early moments of your call are determined in part by conventional teleselling practices. Telephone courtesy demands that you first introduce yourself and your company. The next requirement, stating the purpose of the call, will be fulfilled by your attention-grabber. You can, in fact, employ a *lead-in statement* to make the transition from your introduction and attention-grabber to the body of your call by stating your purpose immediately. There are several ways of doing this:

1. *Make a third-party reference*: "I'm calling at the suggestion of our mutual acquaintance, Bill Johnson, who tells me you're looking for ways to cut the cost of your heating bills."

2. *Follow up on literature sent to the prospect*: "I'm calling to follow up on the literature you requested to determine which of our marketing-support functions can best produce the results you desire."

3. *Refer to a recent advertisement or article you saw about the prospect or his company*: "I read with interest about your experiments in increasing worker productivity. Handi-Mate, our stand-alone work station, reduces assembly time by making everything a worker needs available at one location, eliminating travel from one station to another for tools or parts."

4. *Base the opening on a known industry problem*: "I'm calling to make you aware of our Push-Button Pilot, which eliminates the need for a continuously burning pilot light in your laundromat's dryers, saving you money while conserving energy."

5. *Relate your product to a point made by a prominent national or industry authority*: "Mr. Jackson, Kendra Roberts of the Harte Department Stores recently said that the key to increased sales is better merchandising of multiple options. Is that a marketing problem for your stores?" Go on to point out, "With our unique Retail-Plan Software, you are able to plan, install, and track inventory turnover instantaneously, maximizing both the consumer's options and your profitability."

Some of these examples introduce another key feature of your opener, the *initial benefit statement* (IBS). It was pointed out earlier that the most effective attention-grabber includes a mention of the benefit to the prospect in buying your product. The IBS does that and a little more. It consists of three elements in one sentence: (1) mention of your product by name, (2) a statement of what's in it for the prospect, and (3) proof in the form of features that deliver the benefit. Go back through the five examples of lead-in statements. Separate out any IBSs that you can.

You'll find an IBS in example 3 (Handi-Mate reduces assembly time by making everything a worker needs available at one location), example 4 (Push-Button Pilot saves money and conserves energy by eliminating a continuously burning pilot light), and example 5 (Retail Plan Software increases sales by maximizing customer options).

To create an IBS for your own selling, you will have to do some homework. What matters to the types of prospects you are going to call? The answer to that question can come from your prior experience with similar prospects. If you are entering new markets, read news and general articles or ads for related products to determine what is important to the person you'll be calling. Another source of such information can be third-party referrals.

Your opening comments should be businesslike. Joking or frivolous comments could be interpreted as talking down to the prospect or could indicate that you don't take what you are doing seriously. Be friendly and have confidence in yourself, but don't get cocky or mistake a prospect for a friend. Your positive attitude and conviction of the value of what you do should be apparent. Know and believe in your products, too.

Some telesellers apologize to the prospect for taking up their time, especially in their opening. Don't do it! An apology will be interpreted negatively, putting you on the defensive. Besides, there is no need to apologize if you believe in what you are doing. For your prospects to make intelligent buying choices and derive satisfaction and fulfillment from them, they need to be told the value of your products.

Finally, let your enthusiasm show from the very beginning. You have a lot to be enthusiastic about: You are offering a valuable product. You represent a first-class company. You are a well-trained professional teleseller. These facts should result in your being high on yourself, which will give you a tremendous psychological edge.

Use the examples that were presented in this section to start thinking about the types of things you are going to say to attract attention.

CREATING YOUR OWN ATTENTION-GRABBERS

Both tellesellers who conduct their calls extemporaneously and those who work from a memorized or read script must write out, memorize, and rehearse their opening remarks. Developing and practicing a variety of these openers, so you can choose the best one for each prospect and situation, will get your calls off to a good start.

To begin creating effective openers for your selling situations, review the various categories of attention-grabbers on pages 64–65. Which of these (interest-creating, complimentary, or startling statements, key questions, or analogies) is best suited to your personality and selling situation? Choose one or two to work with initially. But remember, one of the benefits of direct-response marketing is your ability to test the effectiveness of various techniques. Review your work regularly to see where you can make improvements.

Next, establish a profile of the prospects with whom you will be talking. What can you say to each prospect that will get attention? Look for guidance to their problems, concerns, needs, or desires. Research each situation and environment to provide insights. As you talk with a prospect, be alert for further signals. You learn as you go along.

Finally, examine your company's products. What benefits are suitable for you to use in your opening remarks? How will each benefit vary from prospect to prospect? Again, test several statements to see which ones work best. The challenge is to come up with attention-grabbing statements that pack the most punch in the fewest words (remember, you have only twenty seconds). Chapter 12 has useful tips on word choice and use.

Now, write out as many attention-grabbing opening comments as you can (up to about twelve) to test and use on the telephone. Then make sure you've included:

- Your name

- The name of your company

- The purpose of your call

- An IBS

To review: Begin each call with a cheery "Hello!" Introduce yourself and your company. Then concentrate on getting the prospect's undivided attention with an effective attention-grabber. Generate interest in hearing what it is you have to say; snap your listener away from a preoccupation with other concerns. With your opening statement, set the tone for the whole call.

ON YOUR OWN

1. Equip yourself with the attention-grabbing opening comments you have created, a telephone (either real or a toy), and a tape recorder.

2. Rehearse your attention-grabbers until they are memorized.

3. With your recorder nearby and set to "record," hold the telephone handset to your mouth, imagine a prospect on the other end of the line, and make your first attention-grabbing statement. Rewind and replay. How did you sound? Was what you said understandable? Was it exciting? Can you envision it grabbing the prospect's attention? Make revisions as necessary.

4. Repeat the process with each of your attention-grabbers until you are satisfied with how each one sounds.

		Yes	No
SELF-INVENTORY	1. I plan what I am going to say before I get my prospect on the telephone.	—	—
	2. My opening remark successfully grabs the prospect's attention.	—	—
	3. I use various attention-grabbers, each tailored to the product I am selling and to the specific situation.	—	—
	4. My attention-grabbers include mention of at least one key product benefit.	—	—
	5. I get the time I need to conduct the full call that I planned.	—	—

6   Analyze

THE KEY

Before you can present your product as something that will satisfy a prospect's needs, you must know what those needs are. If you plan to use a scripted presentation, you draw on your research and experience before the call to profile a prospect's needs. If you plan extemporaneous presentations, you use questions during the call to determine the prospect's needs and desires. In either case, you will close sales in proportion to how well you have analyzed a person's needs and sold product benefits to meet them. This chapter will increase your understanding of why needs analysis is so important to effective teleselling and will help you learn how to present your products in the best terms possible.

WHY ANALYZE NEEDS?

You analyze a prospect's needs so you can select the appropriate product from your line and present it in terms that satisfy those needs. To quickly and accurately determine those needs, you ask questions and listen to all the prospect says. The more products you sell or the more optional features your products have, the more you will need to analyze before you can present your products in their best light.

If you sell only one product, you still want to learn which product features and benefits will excite each individual prospect—the nature of your analysis changes, but not the analysis itself.

Now that you've grabbed your prospect's attention and interest, what is next? An inexperienced teleseller will think, "Aha! Now I'll sell my product." Having reached this conclusion, he will jump right into a presentation and probably lose the sale. So why would he do that? A beginner may be nervous and want to hide that fact by sounding authoritative. He will go to something he knows well: the product. Or he may be eager to succeed and think the only way to do that is to get in there and *sell*. But, as this teleseller gains experience, he will come to know the value of needs analysis. He will discipline himself to learn what his prospect wants before he tries to sell what he has. And if you, too, go into a sales presentation without analyzing what your prospect wants or needs, your chances of closing the sale are slim. Once you realize this, you won't think of skipping this step in your call strategy.

Qualifying

Analyzing a prospect situation to determine needs, known as *qualifying*, actually began before you contacted the prospect. When you generated leads by matching call lists to product, you were identifying suspects by presumed needs. The process continued when you were cold calling: You gave priority to all those suspects, thereby developing a list of prospects. If you sell to people who initiate the contact, a certain part of the initial analysis was done by them when they reached the decision to call you. Now that you have that prospect on the telephone and paying attention to you, you can analyze for the specific needs and desires your product can satisfy. Your job is to further refine, through questions and listening, whether this particular prospect is going to become a buyer. Is this prospect qualified to benefit from what you are selling? You must now establish in your mind and theirs what their needs are.

The analysis segment of your call strategy is another step in your systematically directing the conversation to a natural close. Go back to the model presented on page 39. Remember, the single most important factor in your prospects' reaction to you is the interest you show in them—in their problems, needs, and concerns. You began to demonstrate that interest when you made your opening comment. Your needs analysis carries you even further into the confidence of the prospect. That is only one of the several important reasons to qualify a prospect before launching into a sales presentation. Some other reasons are the following:

1. Most important, this phase of the interview is intended as the place and way to determine how your products fit the prospect's needs and desires.

2. In those situations where you have a number of appropriate products or your product has a number of optional features to tailor its usefulness, you will need to know more about the prospect and the prospect's situation before you can make a buying recommendation.

3. Questions that build interest in your product can create or increase a prospect's need or desire for your product.

4. Knowing what the prospect wants and needs enables you to build a sales presentation that creates a desire to buy.

5. The basics can quickly be determined. Are you talking to the decision maker? If so, is that person in a position to buy at this time? Such things as budget cycles, the evaluation process, and a group buying decision process can influence whether you want to continue the call you are making.

6. In certain selling situations, you may have to determine whether a prospect can buy from you at all. For example, if you are the distributor of appliances to retail outlets, you cannot sell products to individuals who may contact you. Your agreement with your customers—the retail outlets—precludes that. Or your outbound teleblitz may inadvertently bring you into contact with a customer already buying from one of your company's territory-dedicated tellers or from an outside salesperson.

7. You will learn whether your prospect has the ability to pay. If the product cannot either be paid for outright or financed, there will be no sale. When you sell large-scale items with high price tags, your marketing policy might include rigid financial guidelines for you to follow. Consumer tellers often have to determine family income levels or cash availability before they can proceed to close a sale. In either case, you have to learn from your records and from the prospect whether she can afford your product. If not, it is time for a polite good-bye, and on to the next prospect.

8. The information you gain can help you anticipate and, thus, minimize the number and intensity of objections that will arise.

9. You will implant in the mind of the prospect the idea that you are indeed an expert, because you know what to ask and how to get at what really matters. The prospect's confidence in you will grow accordingly.

10. Your professional integrity is enhanced in the prospect's eyes when you make the right product recommendation.

Creating Desires

Beyond your ability to analyze needs, you want to be able to create buying desires that did not exist prior to your call. "Desires" differ from "needs" primarily in the perception of the prospect. Develop *questions* like the following to ask during your analysis to create the desire to buy:

1. How much could you save in a year, Mr. Brandt, if we cut 30 percent of your home heating bill each month?

2. Would you sleep easier knowing Master-Guard windows were impossible to penetrate from the outside?

3. How would you use the three extra hours a week you'd save with our home-pickup-and-delivery laundry service?

Because desires grow from emotional bases—the absence of a real need is outweighed by an impulse to have—creating desires is an activity more characteristic of consumer teleselling than of business-to-business sales. But don't sell the role of emotion short in *all* buying decisions. A review of the buying considerations and motives mentioned in Chapter 2 should persuade you anew of how important emotion and perceived need are in reaching a buying decision. The three sample questions given and similar ones will help you persuade your prospect to buy at the end of the call.

You might encounter people who are impatient with the analysis process. When you do, and you feel they are qualified to buy, point out how a thorough analysis will benefit them: First, it helps them to clarify their thinking and give priority to their own needs. Second, it helps you recommend only the most appropriate product, options, or configurations, those that are best suited to their needs. And, third, it saves time, both during the call and later, by minimizing the chance of their receiving a product that doesn't do what is needed or wanted.

Recall from Chapter 4 that, in selling, the odds are overwhelmingly against you. If you were to work at random, you would close one sale in 450 calls. Throughout your work, you strive to better those odds. And needs analysis is an integral part of such a strategy. When properly employed, it increases your chances of closing a sale. Keeping that in mind, don't shortcut the analysis of your prospect's needs.

HOW TO ANALYZE NEEDS

If you have been following the procedures advocated here, you already know a little about your prospect. Qualifying began before you initiated contact and continues in the earliest phases of your call. Such factors as why you contact whom you do, your company's marketing strategy, and a profile of existing customers have together identified a segment of the universe at large. Your prospects could be targeted by age, geographic location, income level, sex, or home, car, stereo, or TV ownership, to name a few characteristics. Industrial tellsellers could concentrate on geographic territories, type of industry (those SIC #s), or level of business size, sales, or sophistication.

This prescreening activity, therefore, has been done and is not the qualifying you're concerned with in your on-the-telephone interview. Either those factors are now beyond your control, or the needed influences have already worked. You now want to prepare for the moments when you have the desired prospect on the telephone.

But there is no substitute for your person-to-person exchange with the prospect as the backbone of your needs analysis. The subsequent form that all other steps in the call strategy take depends on it. It is here that the sales call comes to life. Like a gold prospector, you are panning to gather in the nuggets you know are there. You will interact with the prospect, demonstrating your interest in her problems and concerns. You are setting the stage for providing information that points out the proven benefits of what you are selling, information that will enable you to close the sale.

First, before you create your strategy, review the objective of your call. Objectives for a one-call-to-close interview are different from those in a planned three-calls-to-close campaign. Other factors affecting your objectives are your product and your market. If you sell consumer goods, you will probably place more emphasis on creating a need or desire to buy than you would in selling goods to an organization. It may be a more emotional sale, perhaps of a product that doesn't fill any basic need. The same problem faces those business-to-business tellsellers who work with such intangibles as training programs, consulting services, or word-processing software. In any case, you may have to create a need or desire to buy that is not initially apparent to the prospect.

To analyze and determine prospect needs before you get on the telephone, consider the data you may already have on the prospect. If the individual wrote to you, look at the information that was provided, with an eye to screening out inappropriate products. Also look for information gaps that you will need to fill during the call. Don't assume anything or generalize about missing data. You want to show prospects that you have their needs, concerns, and interests at heart. You can't do that if you jump to conclusions before contacting them.

Before launching into the analysis, you should know what factors will knock a prospect out of consideration. These "knock-out" factors prevent wasting time with a dead-end prospect. Depending on the marketing context of your call, the knock-out factors can vary from short but specific (for cold-call teleblitzing to generate leads) to long but general (to better determine what specific products to present and close on). Such factors as "must be a homeowner," "has preschool-age children," or "present insurance expires in 60 days" could screen a consumer in or out. In the business-to-business market, knock-out factors could be credit rating, volume of sales, specific business activity, and the potential size of the order. List here those factors in your marketing guidelines that disqualify potential buyers:

1. _____

2. _____

3. _____

4. _____

5. _____

Qualifying a Prospect

Now that you are ready to begin qualifying a prospect, there are four ways to do it: (1) *using data available on company forms, or using those forms as a guide*; (2) *asking open-ended questions*; (3) *asking closed questions*; and (4) *listening effectively*. You can use these individually or in any combination to get what you need to present your product and close the sale.

1. *Using available data.*   You gathered data through established channels: application forms, orders, requests for information, and the like. They are a good source to guide to you in determining what makes a qualified prospect. Look for the specific information you will need to gather. Look at the forms you will be using (or designing). What do they tell you? List the ways in which these forms can assist you in your analysis:

   1. _____

   2. _____

   3. _____

   4. _____

   5. _____

2. *Asking open-ended questions.*   After you have reviewed this information, you can ask open-ended questions to induce the prospect to give a full, expository answer—not just a yes, no, or other short response. Open-ended questions begin with such words as "what," "when," "how," "where," and "which," and they are intended to get prospects to discuss their needs, problems, and concerns with you. Use open-ended questions when you want a lot of information of a general nature. A mailing list broker, for example, might ask, "What factors are important to you in selecting lists of prospects for your telemarketing operation?" The information you gather using this type of question can then be used to pose additional questions, for example, "You say you look for prospects who bought a related product recently. Are there any criteria about the purchase that are important to further screening?" And while the prospect is talking, you are noting needs, clues to buying motives, concerns, and opportunities to stress a benefit.

   Think about your qualifying situations and list some of the *open-ended* questions you are apt to pose during the call:

   1. _____

   2. _____

   3. _____

   4. _____

   5. _____

3. *Asking closed questions.*   Closed questions are direct and call for a short answer, like yes, no, not over $4,500. Closed questions begin with such words as "do," "has," "can," "will," and "should." "Do you have room on your shelves to take advantage of our quantity discount, Mrs. Wafer?" is such a question. The advantages of the closed question include enabling you to get through data collection rapidly and filling in gaps left by answers to open-ended questions. They also help bring a talkative prospect, the kind who seems to go on forever, under control. Finally, your open-ended questions might have uncovered some unanticipated needs on which you need more data so as to prepare your sales message and stress appropriate benefits—closed questions get that data.

   Think again about the qualifying you will do and list some of the *closed* questions you might ask.

1. _____

2. _____

3. _____

4. _____

5. _____

    With practice, you can make the ultimate use of closed questions by phrasing them in such a way that the other party *has* to answer yes. The prospect gets in a pattern of agreeing with you. That can be indispensable when you get to the close and the prospect finds he has to agree with you once again, acknowledging that your product meets his needs. Although clearly most suited to simple, one-call-to-close situations, it is a valid technique to consider as you plan your questions while analyzing a prospect's needs.

    In addition to gathering information, the questioning technique gets the prospect to interact with you and participate in the sale. That builds interest in your product and confidence in you, both of which are essential in the successful selling situation. And, prospects' answers will provide you with insights into their thinking and their likely reaction to your upcoming presentation.

    The answers you get to the questions you ask help you diagnose needs. It is your responsibility to develop your own list of needs-analysis questions for each product you represent and each prospect situation you encounter. Once you have the information these questions elicit, you are in a position to develop an effective action-getting presentation.

4. *Listening effectively.*   The final key to analysis is to listen to all a prospect is saying—prospects will probably tell you things about themselves and their situation that further clarify your understanding of their needs, concerns, and desires. Listening closely and interpreting the answers help determine what benefits to stress in your selling message. Just as important, you need to listen for buying motives, the factors that will influence the buying decision. These opportunities might not arise in the course of formal questioning.

    Use the data you gather to plan the order in which you will stress the benefits of your product. Determine what is most important to the prospect, and plan to immediately and continually reinforce the information on how your product meets those needs. Less important factors will have to be dealt with in your presentation, but with less emphasis. And what factors are unimportant? To someone with a robot assembly line, for example, the improved worker morale your machine fosters would be of little interest. Skip everything about your product that does not address specific needs of individual prospects.

Finally, listen to learn more about your market and your competitors. Suppose, for example, you want to set up a presentation of your superior customer service. You might ask, "How are your orders handled by your present supplier?" The answer might give you not only insight into how important customer service is to the prospect, but also information about your competition. And it might uncover some heretofore unknown problem your product or company can solve.

Listening, therefore, becomes as important a skill as phrasing the proper questions. Don't ask good questions and then miss the full answers. By listening to all a prospect has to say, whether in answer to your questions or in casual conversation, you will be able to pick up additional hints and information on what the prospect will be looking for in making a buying decision. Listen closely, and hear not just the words being spoken, but the hidden meanings they may carry as well.

The art of asking questions to elicit needed responses is a technique used by every successful teleseller. This is not the idle kind of questioning that accompanies friendly conversation (although that is the effect you are trying to create). Sales-directed questioning requires both planning and thought in order to be effective. You are trying to guide and direct this conversation to your goal: a closed sale. The answers to your questions help you diagnose your prospect's needs. They provide data and give you insights you will need in assembling and delivering your presentation and in asking for the order.

WHAT DO YOU NEED TO KNOW?

The starting point of an effective analysis is this question: "What do I need to know about my prospect—her wants, needs, desires, concerns, or problems—for me to be able to make an appropriate product recommendation?" Someone selling supplies to owners of photocopy machines, for example, will need to know how many machines are installed, what sizes of paper are used, how many copies are made over a given period of time, what methods of delivery are preferred, and more.

To begin planning for this phase of your calls, think of a specific product you are going to sell. In the space provided, describe the ideal prospect for this product. To continue the example of selling supplies for photocopiers, qualities of the ideal prospect might include: being a small to midsize business; making purchase decisions locally (if part of a larger organization); using standard-sized copies ($8\frac{1}{2}$" × 11" and $8\frac{1}{2}$" × 14"); being located within a 50-mile radius of your store (that's how wide a delivery area your trucks cover); and the like. Draw on your product information, advertisements your company has created for the product, your experience with similar prospects (or the experience of others in your work unit if you are new to your job), and so on, to identify the qualities of the ideal prospect for the product you selected for this activity.

_____

_____

_____

_____

_____

_____

_____

_____

_____

_____

_____

Now turn your attention to the questions you need to ask to learn this information. Employ a variety of open-ended and closed questions. Ask questions that will build interest in what you are going to recommend. If possible, include questions that will make the prospect aware of a need he did not recognize previously. In the space provided or on a separate sheet of paper, create a list of all the questions you will need to ask to gain a full understanding of the prospect's needs:

_____

_____

_____

_____

_____

_____

_____

_____

_____

_____

_____

_____

You should now have before you a planned needs analysis—one which, when you are on the telephone with a prospect and have secured answers to the questions you've created, enables you to advocate a specific, appropriate product that will satisfy the needs you've uncovered.

ON YOUR OWN

1. Select one specific prospect, either from the accounts assigned to you or at random from the white or yellow pages of a telephone directory.

2. Repeat the exercise you just completed in the section entitled "What Do You Need to Know?"

SELF-INVENTORY		Yes	No
	1. I think of myself as a problem solver.	____	____
	2. I gather the prospect information I need before making my sales presentation.	____	____
	3. I ask questions to determine my prospect's needs and desires.	____	____
	4. My analysis is intended to also *create* a need or desire to buy.	____	____
	5. I empathize with my prospect as I conduct my analysis.	____	____

7 Advocate

THE KEY

You want to advocate the product you've chosen—the one that best fills the prospect's needs or meets his desires—in a way that gets sales action. You must learn to methodically build your presentation around benefits that show the prospect your product does what is needed and desired. If the call is going to lead to a sale, there must be no doubt in the prospect's mind that your product is desirable and will deliver what is promised. This chapter shows you what goes into a sales-getting presentation and how to develop presentations for use in selling your own products.

ADVOCATE EXTEMPORANEOUSLY

To this point, you have established a call objective and a strategy to help achieve the objective. You have gotten your prospect's attention and, through questioning and attentive listening, analyzed what the person's needs are. You are now ready to advocate a product that you believe satisfies those needs and to do it in a manner that gets sales action. In order to do that, you want to be prepared for any eventuality. By developing broad outlines for presentations that cover most of the situations you are likely to encounter, you will be in a position to construct and deliver a well-thought-out presentation, one that does not come across as a canned pitch.

Contrary to popular opinion—that selling on the telephone is characterized by scripted sales messages—many tellers use a loosely planned, segmented sales presentation when advocating their products. Such a presentation might include some memorized elements, such as five key product benefits or three common product applications in specific situations. But overall, the professional teleseller advocates a specific product in a spontaneous, extemporaneous manner, taking into consideration such factors as the prospect's needs, desires, personality type, and decision-making process.

Among the benefits to you of an extemporaneous presentation are that it can:

- Demonstrate your interest in the prospect.

- Enable you to tailor each call to exact prospect needs.

- Make it easier for you to adapt to marketing changes without having to retrain or rewrite everything before getting on the telephone.

Clearly, then, the recommendation is that, when you advocate your product as a solution to the prospect's needs, you employ an extemporaneous strategy to produce a presentation that appears to be customized and informal but that is in fact precise and rehearsed.

To be effective—to lead to an order—a sales presentation must answer every question the prospect wants answered. Further, it must do so in an orderly manner. To get on the path to an effective advocacy of your product(s), create a list in the space provided or on a separate sheet of paper of all the questions a typical prospect will want to have answered by your presentation. Be specific—instead of writing "The price," break it down into "How much is a basic model?" "What options might be necessary to make it do what I need done?" "How much will those options add to the price?"

_____

_____

_____

_____

_____

_____

_____

_____

_____

Now go back over your questions and number them in the "orderly manner" in which they should be answered. Clues as to what constitutes an orderly manner come from two sources. First, there are the conventions of the markets or industries to which you are selling. Accuracy, for example, is likely to be a concern to anyone considering using a temporary employee agency specializing in accounting and finance professionals. As a result, early on you'd stress your agency's thorough background check and in-house training of those it retains. On the other hand, price, almost always a concern to buyers, might not even come up if you are teleselling a textbook to a professor (after all the student, not the professor, buys the book).

A second clue is contained in what the prospect says. Either overtly or covertly, the prospect identifies the order in which he thinks things are important. One clue is in how often the prospect repeats or reveals concern over an issue. The prospect who keeps asking for assurance that you can deliver the product on schedule is saying that on-time delivery is important. Similarly, the prospect who promptly ticks off a list of concerns—for example, "I'm looking for a supplier who will offer me immediate availability, prompt delivery, and a competitive price"—reveals that she has given the matter some thought and has established an order to her buying motives. In this case, your presentation should stress, in order, your extensive inventory, you fleet of delivery vehicles, and your "guaranteed lowest prices" policy.

As a trained, professional, situation-responsive teleseller, you want to develop and perfect the ability to create flexible, planned sales presentations—action-getting messages that lead to the prospect's wanting to buy—that are delivered extemporaneously.

THE ELEMENTS OF A PLANNED PRESENTATION

You know that the most important factor in prospects' reactions to you is your interest in their needs and concerns. You best demonstrate that interest when you make your product recommendation. This is your opportunity—building on the rapport, integrity, and believability you've developed thus far in the interview—to show your interest in and understanding of the prospect by advocating your product in terms of his needs.

Planning is essential for an action-getting sales presentation. Planning what you will say lets you have more influence over the course of the call. It ensures that you cover all the points important to a prospect. Planning will give you the confidence needed to overcome nervousness and eliminate poor speech mannerisms. And with planning you will have maximum impact on the call's outcome: the achievement of your selling goal.

With the volume of calls you handle, you don't have time to carefully plan out and rehearse each sales message individually. Nor do you need to. Most of your presentations will be similar, and it is neither necessary nor appropriate to think up new messages and strategies each time you handle a call. You don't read your operator's manual each time you get into your car. Similarly, the way in which you stress a benefit, guide the conversation, and secure buyer agreement is suitable for use in most teleselling situations. By planning in advance, you can respond to the vast majority of the situations that arise in the calls you handle.

Finally, knowing in advance the broad outlines of what you are going to say will give you the freedom to listen for that unique combination of prospect needs that each selling opportunity presents. You can be creative in building your presentation in a short period of time by using the elements from your preplanned sales message that you deem appropriate.

There is a natural break in the call-flow pattern as you wrap up your analysis of needs. You have been gathering data, singling out specific needs, refining your understanding of the situation. You will know, and your prospect will sense, when you have gathered the information you need and are ready to move from the analysis to a presentation. You have reached that point when your training, experience, and intuition tell you that you can confidently select the one product that gives the best chance of closing the sale.

When you are advocating your product recommendation, you can follow a basic format that broadly applies to each sales-message outline you develop. This leaves you free to plug in appropriate statements stressing benefits specific to the particular prospect. It is, in fact, sales presentation in miniature, consisting of:

- An attention-getting opening comment.

- The transition statement that carries your prospect from the general opener and needs analysis to specifics relevant to her.

- The body of the presentation.

Your goal, then, is to have planned teleselling messages, brief outlines of what you will say, arranged in a tentative order, for each major segment of the presentation. And remember, you want to build those segments around benefits to the prospect. For example, you will have an outline for effectively presenting the "guaranteed lifetime renewal protection" feature of your automobile insurance policies as a benefit your analysis showed to be important to the prospect. It will consist of the three steps mentioned. You should make a similar outline for each product benefit you identify. Either all of them together or a select number of them will be the basis for your advocacy of your product.

There are a number of reasons (in the form of benefits) why the prospect should want to buy your product. While certain benefits may be available from competitors, and all are usually available individually elsewhere, your particular combination is what makes you unique. And it gives you a strong marketing message to deliver. You want to tell your prospect the company's story and to stress the unique opportunity of doing business with the only source in the marketplace for this combination. List as many benefits as you can think of that, when added up, equal the unique product available only through you and your company. Note how you might phrase these benefits in such a way as to use them when advocating your product recommendation.

1. _____

2. _____

3. _____

4. _____

5. _____

This list adds up to the compelling reason your product is desirable. Did you remember to include yourself as one of the benefits your company offers? If not, you'll want to pay particular attention to Chapter 14.

The sum of the benefits you have listed is what makes your offering unique. The combined package is available only from you, regardless of the price.

ADVOCATING THE APPROPRIATE PRODUCT

In teleselling, having a well-thought-out plan for each segment of your presentation enables you to tell your story in a spontaneous, natural, enthusiastic manner in the time allowed.

Opening Statements

Your first objective in the presentation is to renew the prospect's attention to the purpose of your call. That may have become obscured as you worked through your analysis. As with your initial attention-grabber, your goal is to arouse interest and create a desire to hear more. It takes forethought and effort to make effective attention-getting comments. And there are a number of ways to do it.

You can begin by asking a series of questions. Each question serves to get, build, and keep the prospect's attention. A teleseller of office supplies might do this by asking (after determining that cost saving is a need of the prospect), "How many dollars would you save if I can arrange a Constant Customer Credit Account that reduces your costs by as much as 23 percent?" A person selling home improvements to a consumer who said convenience was a key need might ask, "Would you invest in a total home security system that can be initiated from your bedside, installed with only a screwdriver, and priced competitively with other less sophisticated systems?"

You can also use questions to summarize needs. The insurance teleseller does this by beginning her presentation: "Do I understand correctly that you want coverage that offers adequate protection in a high-inflation economy, that has convenient claims service, and that carries lifetime renewal protection? Is that right, Mr. Roper?" This kind of questioning confirms your understanding of the prospect's needs and desires. You are getting the prospect to participate in your presentation by answering yes—the beginning of an oral contract between you and the prospect to share in the outcome of the call. And you are ensuring that the other party will want to listen with interest to what you are about to say.

Another way to initiate your presentation is to tell about the experience of a customer whose needs or situation is similar to that of your prospect. Your laundry home-pickup-and-delivery service has saved time and money for many of the prospect's neighbors, people just like her. (Mention names here if you have your customers' permission to do so. If not, get that permission.) The situation to which you refer should clearly be relevant to the prospect, and its conclusion should be pertinent to the points you plan in your presentation and close. Success stories can be especially powerful. A textbook teleseller can generate interest and excitement by opening his presentation with a statement describing how another school district's use of his basic-reading-text package resulted in a rise in reading scores and retention rates. Show the prospect how your company helped someone with similar needs, which you were able to satisfy.

In the opening part of your presentation, well-told stories, when carefully chosen and free from controversy, can build interest and can secure agreement (spoken as well as unspoken) on the part of the prospect.

Making a dramatic or challenging statement is another technique that starts presentations off with impact. For instance, you might use a statistical analysis, such as, "One out of every two Americans does not have enough coverage to protect herself from personal financial loss in the event of an accident." Or you could set up a hypothetical case you know to exist among companies like the one your prospect represents: "Firms such as yours have lost an average of $3.5 million a year by using security services that do not bond their guards." If you are going to start with a dramatic statement, make it appropriate to the prospect's needs, as determined by your analysis.

As an exercise, choose two or three prospect needs and/or buying motives you encounter (or are likely to) most frequently. For each, choose an attention-getting technique and write out what you would say to begin your sales presentation to that need or those buying motives:

1. _____

2. _____

3. _____

Transition Statements

The presentation starter is a short moment in the call, usually no more than one or two brief sentences. Next you need a short transition statement, one that will aid you in going from the general tone of your opening statement to the specifics you will have to speak on to close the sale or otherwise get the prospect's agreement.

This passage from attention-getting to presentation of product can again be done with questions, stories, or dramatic statements. If you employed a question-asking technique for opening your presentation, you could make your transition by finally asking, "Now, why are these questions important for you to think about when considering our product?" Or you could explain why the statistical statement you made came to mind while you were talking to this prospect: "Our review of your orders with us in the past six months indicates you may soon be facing that problem unless you upgrade your account now." Finally, use a dramatic statement when appropriate: "Based on what you have told me, Mrs. Moore, you will save over $75 a month in fuel costs alone with the newest furnace in our line."

Stop here and build transition statements suitable for use with the attention-getting opening strategies you developed in the preceding section.

1. _____

2. _____

3. _____

The Body of the Presentation

You are at the point now where you are ready to recommend your product for the prospect's consideration. If you have more than one product that fits the prospect's needs, your analysis of needs has told you which one to recommend. If you have only one product for the situation, you will have to choose the most beneficial features of the product for this particular prospect. In either case, everything you have been doing up to this point has been in preparation for what you are going to do and say now. Your presentation has reached the point at which you can pull together all your skills as a teleselling professional—your communication techniques, product knowledge, and persuasive selling skills, enhanced by your enthusiasm and empathy—and advocate what you believe will meet the prospect's needs.

As your conversation with the prospect develops, you should be thinking of how what is being said will fit into and affect your presentation. In that way, when the body of your presentation is before you, you are not grasping at ideas randomly. Rather, you are moving into a planned portion of the call that you will have assembled as your needs analysis unfolded. Your presentation will:

- Include a point-by-point coverage of the needs of the prospect.

- Stress product benefits to the prospect, telling what's in the purchase for him.

- Feature an orientation that emphasizes and demonstrates the fulfillment of the prospect's needs.

Begin by quickly ordering in your mind the most important needs, desires, and concerns of your prospect. If you sense the prospect has a ranking of their order of importance, follow it.

Second in your list are those requirements that, while important, are not the most pressing. These you will address or minimize.

Finally, using a combination of your intuition and experience, set aside discussion of benefits you feel are not important or which may have been false leads.

Equipped with such a ranked list in your mind, you now want to move through it, addressing each point in a way that stresses the benefit to the prospect of buying your product. Review Chapter 2 to refresh yourself on selling product features and advantages as benefits.

Enthusiasm, word choice, pacing, and voice inflection will help you deliver an interesting, forceful message. Keep your talk in sequence, hitting most often the benefits that are most important to the prospect. Bring up other, less important benefits as the opportunity arises. As you gain experience, you will find it increasingly easier to hammer home an effective, enthusiastic, action-getting presentation.

But don't get carried away. Too many high points or too many benefits may confuse your prospect. You don't want to go over a shopping list of every possible benefit you can think of. Limit yourself to the top two or three in the mind of the prospect, and sell them well. Remember that you are building your message to the call's fifth step: asking for an order.

As you cover each benefit, conclude your presentation by showing how it relates directly to the prospect. "Can you see, Mrs. Moore, where you can save $75 a month on heating bills?" "Does the six-hour fulfillment that our automated process guarantees, with toll-free access for you, satisfy your requirement, Mr. Craig?" Secure agreement and move on to your next benefit, or address any objections you encounter (this is discussed in detail in the next chapter).

Advocating your product recommendation comes and goes very quickly. It begins with its own attention-getter. Then you make a transition to the body of your talk, carrying the prospect from the general to her specific situation. Finally, if the prospect voices no objections, as a natural conclusion to the conversation, you must proceed directly to step 5 and ask for the order. That's it. If you are well-prepared, enthusiastic, and empathetic, this will be one of the more rewarding parts of your work. It is just plain exciting to present the right product to the right person in a manner that gets a sale.

ON YOUR OWN

1. Review the questions you posed in the "On Your Own" activity concluding Chapter 6 (page 79). Speculate on how those questions might be answered by the prospect you had in mind (or better yet, contact the prospect—if it was a real person—and conduct a needs analysis).

2. In the natural and logical order called for in this chapter, arrange the features, advantages, and benefits of a product you would recommend to satisfy this prospect's needs.

		Yes	No

SELF-INVENTORY

1. I have planned selling presentations I can tailor to different circumstances as the need arises. ____ ____

2. I assess the buying motivations of each prospect and tailor my presentation accordingly. ____ ____

3. My advocacy of a product occurs in both an orderly and logical manner. ____ ____

4. My presentation to prospects addresses what my product will do *for them*. ____ ____

5. My advocacy creates a need and a desire to buy my product. ____ ____

8 Answer

The Key

Prospects can at any time object to buying your product. If they didn't, your work wouldn't be very challenging. This chapter will help you develop techniques to respond to each type of objection likely to arise in your day-to-day teleselling. It will show you how to set up an Objection Handbook to assist you in being on top of most objections you will encounter.

THE CHALLENGE OF OBJECTIONS

If you have essentially completed the presentation stage of the call, you and your prospect have been cooperating. You have been guiding and directing the conversation and have created in the prospect an assumption of a mutual interest: your product and the prospect's need for it. But when it comes time to ask for the order, you are likely to begin encountering a defensive strategy, one based on objections. Objections are those obstacles, either real or imagined, that stand between you and a closed sale. Learning how to overcome or answer objections and go on to close a sale is a skill fundamental to all teleselling.

The only salesperson who won't encounter an objection is one who is the sole representative of a product that everyone needs to survive. Since that does not describe you, the first realization for you to come to is this: Objections are going to arise. Knowing this, you can get on with the real challenge: answering them and going on to close the sale.

When are you likely to encounter objections? If you include as an objection the screen that you must get through, expect them immediately. And they can occur at any other time during the course of the call as well. The prospect who interrupts your attention-grabber with "I'm too busy now, call me next month!" has hit you with an objection. Other early objections include, "Send me some literature on your product and I'll get back to you," and "I'm not the right person to talk to." You must be ready for objections as soon as you get a prospect on the line.

However, the call flow presented here anticipates that the most likely place for objections to arise is either during the action-getting presentation or when you ask for the order. It is at the latter time that your prospect has to decide whether to buy. Faced with such a decision, your listener will probably begin thinking of the reasons not to buy. As these reasons come to mind, the prospect will present them to you as obstacles preventing him from buying now—or ever.

Remember, though, that this is not always the case. One of the most gratifying moments in selling comes when you have wrapped up your presentation and asked your prospect to buy, and she answers "yes," without hesitation. It happens more frequently than you think. On average, with a soft offer ("If you are not completely satisfied, merely write 'cancel' on the invoice and return it in the postage-paid envelope") you can expect a favorable reaction about two or three times an hour from a qualified list. With a hard offer ("Send it back if you aren't satisfied; we'll refund your money and pay the postage"), one close an hour is a job well done. People do have needs, want products to satisfy them, and buy when so persuaded. As one sales trainer put it, "Sales usually aren't lost. They go to the competition."

Reasons for Objections

Going back to objections, there are a number of reasons why they arise:

1. Some people are simply not open to change or are unwilling to take risks. If your approach and analysis of needs (assuming you got this far with these people) didn't persuade them otherwise, get off the telephone. Experience and empathy will enable you to spot such a prospect, even if it is someone who has participated politely in your call. Once you detect rigidity, disengage.

2. Some people simply object out of habit. For them, saying no is second nature, perhaps developed as a first line of defense against buying anything.

3. Hard as you may find it to believe, some objections arise because of your mistakes. You may not have properly qualified the prospect, and therefore, have presented the wrong product. You may have been misunderstood because you were unclear in your explanation of how the product meets the needs or because you were nebulous about how the prospect will benefit.

4. The prospect may be sincerely interested but vague and evasive in describing needs, making it difficult for you to make a strong presentation. The resulting objections are usually easy to handle, though.

5. You might not have created a sufficient need or desire to buy in the mind of the prospect. She may want to be further convinced that your product will do what you say. She will compare what you have said with what she knows of other, competing, products; she wants to get the best product at the best price from the most appropriate source.

6. Some prospects have legitimate concerns. Because they will have to live with the consequences of a buying mistake for a lot longer than you will, they want a full picture of what they are buying and how it suits their needs.

Kinds of Objections

Objections take different forms, but they mostly fall into four distinct categories:

1. *The stall.* This may be difficult to detect and deal with because it doesn't sound like an objection at all. In fact, it can sound downright positive and make much sense. "Yes, I'm interested. Send me some literature." "We will be deciding that next month. Call me back then." "I have to consult my wife before we make a decision like that. Can we call you back?" Examine statements such as these, which you will hear regularly. Which of them could be just putting you off?

2. *The misunderstanding.* This objection is easily recognized when it arises. The prospect merely didn't understand what you said or misinterpreted it. "But I don't need one right now [which may also mean, 'I can't afford it now']. And it will be sold by the time I do" is such a case, and a golden opportunity to stress a new benefit: your layaway or interest-free deferred-payment plan. The problem you face here is similar to that of a

major league second baseman going after an easy ground ball: Easy as it may seem, if he doesn't do it right, he'll be charged with an error and the batter will be safe. The misunderstanding has to be addressed, as do all other objections. What misunderstandings arise after your presentation? If some occur frequently, rework your benefits outlines in an attempt to prevent them.

3. *The false objection.* You know from experience or from your records that what is said just isn't so. The prospect who says he doesn't need to make a buying decision soon, when you know his existing supply of a product is about to run out, has raised a false objection. When you are sure the objection is false, it may be a warning to you that this prospect is a lost cause. If a prospect continually raises false objections, consider terminating the call and moving on to other, more interested prospects.

4. *The real objection.* Because they are based on facts, such objections must be acknowledged, answered, and closed. They result from the prospect's analysis of her situation and experience in light of what you are presenting. The objection could be to price—perhaps your product really does cost more than a similar product from a competitor—or it could be based on the fact that your product lacks some feature or combination of features that is important to the prospect. You must deal with real objections in a direct, no-nonsense manner, and you will learn how to do so later in this chapter.

Heading Off Objections

As you have seen from the examples, objections can take the form of either questions or declarative statements. And you must be especially sensitive to statements that sound innocuous but are, in fact, objections.

Before turning to specific techniques for handling objections, consider a couple of ways of initially heading them off. First, with a little planning, and a sensitivity to what you will encounter or have encountered on the telephone, you can avoid some of the most frequent or serious objections likely to arise. You can do this with a technique called the *preemptive statement*: You answer the objection before it is voiced.

Consider, for example, that you notice you are getting an increasing number of complaints that your replacement supplies have been very slow to arrive. The result is that existing customers have been going to a competitor for supplies, and, because of your reputation for slow fulfillment (spread by word of mouth), you are experiencing difficulty in getting new customers as well. Assuming you have done something to correct this serious business deficiency, you can now head off the objection that you know will be forthcoming. In this instance, your preemptive statement might occur near the end of your presentation: "Our new, automated fulfillment center, with a twenty-four-hour toll-free number, gives you the assurance that we will ship your order within six hours of receiving it. This new system is state of the art and not only has won recognition in our industry, but has received acclaim from our customers as well." Go on to close the statement with, "If you like, I can send you several recent letters from satisfied customers, testifying to what I am saying." This preemptive statement could also be the reason for your call to past customers, and it could appear as early as your attention-getter when you are calling these people.

In any case, you have defused a major objection. Keep track of your most frequently encountered objections—ones you know can be handled. Develop similar preemptive statements to integrate appropriately into your planned call, and begin deflecting those objections.

One cautionary note—especially relevant to planning your preemptive strategy but applicable throughout your call—concerns that dreaded mental exercise, jumping to conclusions. If you occasionally hear particular objections and you know that they are not based on your product's or company's deficiency, you might conclude that everyone with whom you talk is going to raise these objections. Such a prejudice on your part is dangerous to your sales health. You will, in a defensive mood, either bring up the objection or answer it when the prospect has not thought to make it, and you will have effectively planted in the prospect's mind another reason not to buy. Handling objections that are brought up will keep you busy enough—don't add to your difficulties.

Some objections arise when you least expect them. You want to be ready to deflect these smoothly until an appropriate time in your planned call. This can frequently be done with a comment like, "You've raised an important question, Ms. Walker. In a moment I will walk you through our order-processing procedure, and you will see why you can have every confidence that your order will be in your hands no more than two days after you place it—even earlier at only a slight extra charge if you need air freight service." If you cannot control the conversation to delay objections, you should handle them when they arise, either by jumping to your preemptive statement or by asking the prospect to hold off a few moments. If you employ the latter technique, make a written note of the objection and be sure you come back to it as promised.

Handling Objections

There is nothing wrong with being stumped by an objection the first time you encounter it. This happens repeatedly, even to the best sales people, despite thorough preparation. It is, however, inexcusable to be stumped by that same objection a second time. It means you weren't responsive the first time it arose and didn't give it a second thought. To prevent that from happening, you should begin an Objections Handbook. This is a place for you to write down the key data concerning each objection, and, after you think it through, prepare an answer to it. The form shown in Figure 8.1 can be reproduced either on pages for a loose-leaf notebook or on 5-by-8 note cards, for use in establishing your Objections Handbook.

When you meet an objection that you fail to answer to your complete satisfaction, write it down as soon as you get off the telephone. Then think about what might motivate such an objection: impatience, misunderstanding, an inappropriate buying motive you hadn't anticipated, a real concern for the correctness of what you are saying, or some other factor. Think how you might answer it if it arises again. Consult others to see if they have encountered it and, if so, how they handled it. Also check your product literature to learn benefits you can use to overcome the objection. Finally, formulate a strategy, using the techniques described in the next section of this chapter, to handle the objection the next time it arises. What exactly will you say? Have the answers outlined and within reach at all times or committed to memory.

Adopt the attitude that every objection has an answer and be prepared to answer the objections you are likely to hear. By using your Objections Handbook regularly, in a very short time, you will have noted and planned a response to almost all objections you will encounter.

The following are examples of common objections, taken from situations that occur during the screening out of nonqualified prospects. A prospect might say that:

- She has just bought your product or one just like it.

- She has a large inventory on hand already.

- Your price is higher than that of a competitor.

These are among the many objections that will make an inexperienced teleseller, hearing them while talking with a prospect, conclude there is no sale to be made. Always in search of the "perfect" prospect, the novice will hang up and get on with the next call.

Product:

_____

Objection Encountered:

_____

Where in the Call It Most Frequently Occurs:

_____

Possible Motivations:

_____

Answers:

_____

_____

_____

_____

_____

_____

Balance-Sheet Reply:

_____

_____

_____

_____

_____

_____

FIGURE 8.1. Objections Handbook

In fact, each of these objections, and most others like them, call for some further analysis. Consider these questions in response to the three objections:

1. *The recent purchase objection*: "Are you happy with it? Does it do everything you expected? Do others in your household (or company) have a similar need for one? When will you be replacing it?"

2. *The large inventory situation*: "How fast do you consume your inventory? Can I help you dispose of that inventory [find another suitable user or, in a very aggressive move, buy it to make room for your product]? Do you have room to carry two lines, which will enable you to see which one sells better for you?"

3. *The price complaint*: "Are you getting everything you want or need for that price? Would a product that does more for you be worth a little more to you?"

As you can see, every objection has a response. It may not overcome the objection, but that is not the point. You always want to test each objection with a response to determine if it is real or merely a smoke screen to evade you and the purchase. If after you have given it your best effort you cannot overcome it, then go on to the next call.

MAKING OBJECTIONS INTO QUESTIONS YOU CAN ANSWER

Effectively answering objections requires being prepared in advance. Your Objections Handbook will help you keep on top. Knowing that you are prepared to answer objections as they arise helps you to stay relaxed, confident, and unintimidated by them. You are free to be creative as you deal with each situation and deliver convincing answers.

While real objections are the ultimate challenge and are the primary concern here, the techniques presented are appropriate for handling all objections. Regardless of whether they are stalls, misunderstandings, false, or real, the same general procedures apply: They require only that you adapt them to the type of objection you are confronting.

Five-Step Strategy

When you hear an objection:

1. *Restate* it in the form of a question, like this: "Do I understand you correctly—you are hesitant to act today because you fear that, in the event of an accident, you will have difficulty getting your claim settled?" This tactic accomplishes several things: It shows the prospect you are not afraid of the objection; you are going to confront it head on. Also, you are recapturing the initiative in the call, which momentarily passed to the prospect when he raised the objection. You also want to be sure you fully understand the objection. If you don't, your prospect will no doubt stop you again and explain it further. On hearing the objection restated, the prospect, too, is put at ease. Some of the objection's sting is gone. Finally, you demonstrate the desirability of a meeting of the minds as the two of you work out an answer together.

2. After you have restated the objection, *secure agreement that you are both talking about the same thing* before you proceed. Keep it brief: "Is that correct?" or "Do I understand you correctly?"

3. *Qualify the objection.* Make sure it is a real obstacle to the sale, not just an excuse to put you off. Determine how important it is. Will you have to overcome it, or can you handle it by minimizing it? As during your earlier analysis, you should use questions. The answers you get will allow you to resume the guidance and direction of the call. It is important to the dynamics of selling that you stay on the offensive. Use questions to learn the real reason for the objection. This is especially important in dealing with stalls and false objections, where the motive isn't apparent or reasonable. Ask, "Why do you feel that way about it?" or "How important is that to you?" Questions will make the prospect stop and think. And the dialogue that ensues will give you valuable insights into the prospect's thinking at this point in the interview.

   When you fully understand the objection, you are in a better position to answer it. Look upon this phase of the interview as a sincere effort on the part of both parties to reach an understanding. If your prospect wants and needs your product, and it fills that need, answering objections removes obstacles to closing the sale.

4. Once you have determined that an objection is real, you are ready to *answer* the objection with a mini action-getting presentation. Go back

and re-emphasize a benefit, or introduce new benefits that again meet the needs of the prospect. *Never argue with the prospect.* Instead, employ your most powerful vocabulary and be positive. Use words that inspire trust, that are believable. Resist the temptation to exaggerate or get carried away in your desire to make the sale. Remember, the prospect is constantly evaluating the quality of your information.

And stick to the basics. Continue to concentrate on the need and desire to buy, and spark further interest. You might say, "You are right to be concerned about claim service, Mrs. Wolcott. I am pleased to say our claim service is fast, efficient, and easy to call on if needed. We are available twenty-four hours a day, from anywhere in the United States."

Some objections, however, simply cannot be overcome. Perhaps the prospect has a long and very satisfying buying relationship with your competitor. In such an instance, you can handle the objection by using the *balance-sheet technique* (borrowed from the accounting profession): You play up the pluses of your product and play down its minuses. You could, for example, say, "In the long run, don't our benefit A and benefit B present an attractive alternative to the product you are now using, making us the desirable choice at this time?" Avoid criticizing your competitor, but do concentrate on minimizing the importance of their benefits. The enthusiasm you have for your own company and product plays a strong role. You have to believe that what you offer is better than what the prospect already has. You may want to write out a balance-sheet reply to each objection listed in your Objections Handbook.

5. Finally, after answering an objection or minimizing it, *close on it.* Do this by asking for the prospect's agreement with what you have said. This should be done for each objection individually. If you have presented a sincere, straightforward, and reasonable answer, agreement should not be hard to get. Each agreement you secure brings you that much closer to the sale.

Remember: In every case, you want to follow the clean, professional process of restating, qualifying, addressing, and securing agreement on each objection the prospect puts in your path.

A word is in order about the role of your marketing strategy in countering objections. If you find that objections you cannot answer continue to block sales, change strategies—make a special offer. If you have sufficient authority, you might want to seek out and offer the prospect a *premium* for buying. The premium should be of a related nature, such as a free first issue to periodical subscribers, a month's supply of a favorite home product to those using your housecleaning service, or a coupon good for $50 worth of gasoline to those leasing their car from you. Another tactic is the *discount pricing* strategy: "Act now and you save 25 percent off the full price of the product." The discount should be substantial enough to make buying attractive—at least 10 percent. A third tactic, to use either by itself or in conjunction with your premium or discount, is setting *a deadline* for a special offer: "This is sent to you for a free 30-day examination before you pay the invoice or you can return the product" or "This offer is good only until the end of the month." Again, the length of the deadline should be reasonable for the situation. Setting short deadlines to capitalize on people's absent-mindedness or busy schedules will be spotted immediately by today's sophisticated prospect.

If you are working for a company, of course, you may not have the authority to establish such marketing strategies. In that case, go to your management, fully explain why such a policy needs to be established, and seek approval for implementing special offers to induce prospects to set their objections aside.

AND WHAT ABOUT THE PRICE OBJECTION?

Some of the most frequently encountered objections are to price: "Your price is too high" or "I can't afford it right now" or "Your competition is cheaper." Telesellers in all businesses hear this frequently, whether dealing with individual consumers or professional buyers, and you have to learn to address it.

You should not be surprised that you employ the same technique for answering the price objection as you do for answering all other objections. Begin by restating the objection. It is especially important to ensure that it isn't based on a misunderstanding, either of the savings to be realized by the prospect if they will use your product or of your pricing structure. A misunderstanding could lead them to incorrectly conclude that they will be paying a price higher than the one called for by your pricing strategy. Many price objections are based on a misunderstanding.

If it is a real objection, however, you want to assume the attitude that price is, in fact, a reflection of the value received. The larger the gap between the price you are asking and the value perceived by the prospect, the more often the price objection will arise. If your product is in fact overpriced, you will have a hard time overcoming price resistance. From the start of your call, you should build the perception of value received.

But what if your price is fair? In that case, let your prospect know that you, your company, and the fine products and services you provide are all part of that price. If it accurately reflects the product's value, you should once again be selling benefits. And what benefits (or value) are you selling?

- *The product itself.* All of the tangible and intangible benefits that you have found in your product research.

- *What the product does for the prospect.* In selling terms, the satisfaction of whatever buying motives the prospect may have.

- *Your company.* The reputation that stands behind the product. You may even want to integrate into your presentation some information on your company, its strength and history of success, if this will be a factor in your sale.

- *The service you offer to customers with the product.* Anything from a money-back guarantee to a full-service staff that ensures customer satisfaction.

- *You.* An inherent part of the purchase. You are an important part of the sale, for all of the reasons covered earlier and later in this book. Your importance cannot be minimized, ever—and it is especially important to answering the price objections.

ON YOUR OWN

1. Return once again to the prospect you used to complete this activity in Chapters 6 and 7. Secure a half-dozen copies of the Objections Handbook form found on page 97.

2. Write out as many objections as you can that the prospect in question is likely to raise, one on each page of your Objections Handbook.

3. Using the five-step strategy presented in this chapter, prepare to answer the most troubling of the objections you wrote down. What would you say, at each step of the process, to effectively answer the objection coming from the specific prospect?

		Yes	No
SELF-INVENTORY	1. I accept objections as a fact of life in teleselling.	____	____
	2. I restate the prospect's objections to insure I understand them.	____	____
	3. I keep a list handy of objections I've encountered previously, with answers to them noted.	____	____
	4. I answer objections with product benefits appropriate to the user.	____	____
	5. After I have answered an objection, I secure agreement by asking a closing question.	____	____

9 Ask

THE KEY

The goal of your entire call is to get action, whether that action is securing an appointment, closing a sale, or committing the prospect to some intermediate action. Throughout each call, be alert for signals that the prospect is ready to act, and be prepared to react to these signals with a trial close. If you have received no such signals by the time you have completed your presentation and answered the objections that arose, you must employ an appropriate technique to close the sale, one that makes the sale a natural conclusion to the call. Whatever technique you employ, it all comes down to asking the prospect to buy. This chapter gives you pointers on how to tell the right time to do so. It presents various techniques for asking for an order, including both trial and final closes, to enable you to select the ones best suited to your call goals and selling situations.

THE CLOSING PROCESS

Closing the sale, or obtaining some similar commitment to action, has been your goal from the start. Now here you are, having worked through the various steps in your call strategy—you approached the prospect to get her attention; you analyzed her needs; you advocated a product to meet those needs; you successfully answered all questions and objections. The next step is to ask for the order.

Many people, despite being well-intentioned about their teleselling career, fail because they are afraid to ask for the order. And yet, if you have correctly covered the steps in the Straight A's selling system, asking for the order and closing the sale should come as the natural result of the conversation you have been having with the prospect. You have been building the entire sales interview to the point of asking for the order. And when the goal of closing a sale guides your call strategy and conversation, and the prospect has stuck with you this far, he expects the next step to be a request to buy.

If asking for the order is such a natural step, why do so many people have difficulty taking it? The most common explanation is fear of rejection: being afraid that, by finally asking the prospect to buy, the teleseller is confronting the ultimate NO of the call. "No, not at this time," the prospect may say. And where do you go from there?

In simplest terms, there are very few people who can successfully sustain themselves on a diet of constant rejection. Asking a person to buy takes a lot of courage when rejection is the overwhelmingly likely result (See Table 4.1, Prospecting as a Numbers Game, if you've forgotten). Being able to respond favorably in that situation, by asking why not and then proceeding to try again, takes both skill and determination. The conversationalist will stop when he hears "No!" The teleseller, trained in product knowledge, selling, and communication skills, tries to turn a "No" into a sale. Expecting and asking a prospect to buy are what marks you as a professional.

Some telesellers lack confidence in the usefulness and value of their product. Or they may not feel the price is fair. Still others have not followed the buying/selling process and, thus, have not secured agreement to benefits statements or have not answered objections. When they get to the final step, they are at a disadvantage and perhaps feel their failure is certain. Any of these attitudes is reflected, in turn, in the closing techniques used. Finally, some haven't really come to see themselves as salespeople and, thus, don't realize that closing sales is a part of the responsibility of their jobs. For all of these reasons, some telesellers freeze at asking for the order.

You are being paid to close sales. Your company needs those sales to continue in business. Your prospect needs the product you are offering, either for work or for personal reasons. You and, if you are a breadwinner, your family need you to close sales, both to produce income and to gain increased satisfaction from your work. So a lot is riding on your ability to ask for the order.

WHEN TO ASK FOR THE ORDER

There are two times when it is natural and appropriate to ask for the order:

1. When you pick up indicators, called "buying signals," that the prospect is willing to buy.

2. When you have completed your presentation and feel that you have answered any objections the prospect has raised.

Fortunately, many prospects tip you off when they are ready to make a buying decision. Throughout each call, you should be on the lookout for buying signals. Such signals can occur at any time during the call, but most frequently they surface either during your presentation (confirming that it is, indeed, action getting) or as you successfully answer any objections presented. If you are generating interest in your product, your prospect will give you signals. They should be taken to mean that it's time for you to ask for the order.

Buying signals can take many different forms, limited only by the products you represent and the type of prospect you are calling on. They are easily recognized, usually surfacing in the form of questions (or statements) that indicate the prospect is envisioning using your product. Buying signals are both specific and directly related to doing business with you. They can be phrased as questions:

- How soon could you make delivery?

- Can I use my credit card to pay for it?

- What would it cost if I didn't take the entire package, only feature A and D?

- How much work is involved in getting it into operation?

- Do you guarantee I'll get my money back if I'm not satisfied?

Just as frequently, buying signals can come in the form of statements:

- I'll bet I could even use it to do [some other function] as well.

- That sounds all right to me.

- I could probably cancel my existing service arrangement the day after your product arrives.

- My neighbor said he'd had good results with your product.

- I've needed something that does this for a long time.

What do *your* prospects say to indicate a willingness to buy? What buying signals can you listen for, or do you plan to listen for, as you handle your calls? Begin a list of them here:

1. _____

2. _____

3. _____

4. _____

5. _____

Learn to listen from a prospect's point of view (empathy again), interpreting her comments to recognize a willingness to buy. And when you detect it, go to a trial close as described in the next paragraph. It either will get you the business or will allow you to further qualify and answer her counterobjection. But always ask for an order when you hear a buying signal.

Suppose the prospect indicates interest by asking, "How soon could you make delivery?" Your thought-out-in-advance response might be, "Do you have your credit card handy? If you'll give me the number and expiration date now, I'll see that it's shipped today so you'll have it before the weekend. Will that be in time for your use?"

If the prospect says "yes," go immediately to your wrap-up and hang-up routine (see page 112). If the prospect says "Well, yes, but I'm not sure I want to buy," you should seize the opportunity to ask why not. That question will stimulate objections. Using strategies developed in your Objections Handbook, secure future agreement by again bringing up appropriate benefits. Your trial close thus accomplishes one of two things: (1) You close the sale; or (2) you hear another objection and have to secure agreement on that point of discussion and try to close again.

Go back to the buying signals you listed earlier. Select several of them, and, for each signal, write out a closing statement that turns it into a trial close.

1. _____

2. _____

3. _____

4. _____

5. _____

HOW TO ASK FOR THE ORDER

For the professional teleseller, asking for the order is not a manipulative activity intended to trick the prospect into buying. It is a strategy for bringing the call to a close with a definitive and favorable buying decision. The alternative is a sales call where the prospect assumes the initiative and says, "I'll think about it and get back to you." *You* want the initiative and must not wait for the prospect to close either the sale or the call.

It is at this critical point in the interview, then, that you must ask the prospect to buy. But you don't, of course, merely blurt out, "Well, will you buy?" There are a number of more subtle, but very effective, techniques you can employ in a smooth, natural manner to get a buying commitment. Review them here to determine which ones will work best for you in the situations you face.

Assume-the-Order Close

One highly recommended technique draws its inspiration from what your attitude should be throughout the call: the *assume-the-order close*. If the call flow indicates a meeting of the minds between you and the prospect and agreement on selling points is frequent, you assume the prospect is going to buy. Some tellers carry this a little further and begin portraying, early in the call, situations wherein the prospect has already made the purchase. Such questions as "Will you use this on all of your trucks or only on those hauling hazardous chemicals?" or "Which of your present components will you replace first with our model?" can carry the cooperative prospect one step further toward the close by assuming the sale is made. Such a technique can be used in conjunction with those buying signals that show the prospect is clearly envisioning the product in use. With a minimum of ceremony and doing nothing to break the mood, you pick up on the signal and carry it through to a close.

Use caution in reading buying signals when using this technique. If you misread the signals and go to the assumptive close, indicating as much in your closing effort, you will come across to the uncommitted prospect as pushy. If, however inadvertently, you make the prospect feel pressured, the result will be the immediate raising of numerous other obstacles to the purchase. Objections then will be hard to overcome. Use your best listening skills, your empathy, and your sensitivity when planning to use the assumptive close. If you do and read the signals correctly, this can be one of your most powerful closing techniques.

Ordering-Instructions Close

A related technique is called the *ordering-instructions close*. When your intuition says the time is right to close, tell the prospect how to follow your ordering procedures. It is as though you were handing your listener a contract to sign or a purchase order to approve. With confidence akin to that demonstrated in your assumptive close, you give instructions on how to initiate the order. It can be as easy as the insurance teleseller's saying, "Now, if you'll just do the following, your coverage will be in effect at midnight of the day we receive your check." If you are selling to a business, you can ask the prospect to get out the company's purchase requisition and then help him fill it in correctly with an order for your product, including specifications, model numbers, catalog numbers, and so on.

Choice Close

Both of the aforementioned techniques are low key, grow out of the course of the call, and assume the prospect is showing signs of making a buying decision. It is, however, often necessary to help the prospect come to the point of making a buying decision. But high-pressure selling usually won't work with today's sophisticated consumer, and it is especially easy to get rid of a pushy teleseller: The prospect just hangs up. Yet pressure-free teleselling is not appropriate either. The middle ground to take is to adopt the attitude that you are helping the prospect make the best buying decision to meet her needs. If your product is, in your opinion, the most suitable one, your firm insistence on the prospect's need to go with that product will often be welcome. When confronted with a prospect who should buy but cannot make a decision, you must take the initiative and urge, encourage, even compel the prospect to act.

For many years the *choice close*—forcing a yes answer by setting up two choices, both of which could only be answered with a commitment to buy— was recommended as a means of helping force a decision. Today, however, prospects—especially professional buyers—may be conditioned to resist this close, which has been overused. That is not to say it is never appropriate, especially as a trial close. But be sure the choices are not contrived just to get the prospect to pick one. If it is natural to present two or more options and such an offer flows from the conversation, use it. An example would be to ask the credit-card customer if four monthly installments or one payment is preferred. When the prospect says he prefers one payment, go on to write the order up.

Offer Close

Another technique that is especially useful in teleselling is the *offer close*. As mentioned earlier, such a close can be an integral part of your marketing strategy and is often called the "soft" offer. You tell the interested prospect, or remind the reluctant one, that there is no risk in trying the product. Hence, a magazine subscription can be offered "free" by telling the prospect, "I'll send you the next month's issue along with the invoice. If you are not satisfied, merely write 'cancel' on the invoice and return it to me." In a related move, appropriate to virtually any item for sale, you can set up a thirty-day money-back guarantee. If the prospect isn't completely satisfied, the item can be returned for a full refund. Or you can offer the option of not having to pay for the product for the first thirty days of ownership.

Ask-A-Question Close

You can also close a sale by *asking questions* to nail down the details of the sale. This technique begins with modified choice questions, such as, "Should we write this up for you with the minimum-purchase-guarantee provision? The amount we have been discussing would qualify you for that special rate" or "What limits of liability coverage do you want on your cars?" When the prospect makes a positive choice, you have the buying signal you need to go on to close the sale.

Summation Close

Still other techniques exist. In the *summation close*, for example, you summarize the needs you've uncovered and show how the benefits of your product meet those needs. With such a strategy, you would proceed by saying, "We have seen that you need the following . . . My product does that for you by . . . The cost to you will be . . . Now let me tell you how to initiate the order." This close is especially powerful in those situations where, throughout the call, you have sensed the prospect's desire for your product. By summarizing the entire situation, you also help lay to rest that phenomenon known as buyer's remorse, the natural feeling a prospect has, immediately after making a buying decision, that she has made a mistake.

Earlier, in the section on handling objections, you were presented with the concept of the balance sheet. It works as a summation-closing technique as well, especially in those instances when you are helping prospects to make up their minds. Walk the prospect through the benefits of the product being offered. Then ask whether it isn't true that the factors favoring your product outweigh those provided by the product currently in use or by that of your competitors. Again, ask for the order when you hear a favorable response.

Learning Closing Techniques

Select the techniques best suited to your selling situation and prospects. Outline one or more closing statements using the techniques you've selected. Repeat them aloud to hear how they sound, or say them into a tape recorder for playback and evaluation. As with other aspects of your call strategy, you want to have your closing statements thought out in advance, planned to be as powerful as possible, and available for immediate use as the need arises.

Learning closing techniques that work is an ongoing process. Talk with your colleagues about what works for them. Read the books on selling listed in Sources for More Information at the back of the book. Look to other selling how-to books as well to pick up tips that apply to your work. Plan to use at least one closing technique in each call you handle, and practice that technique. Most importantly, condition yourself to ask for the order. And don't take the first no for an answer; carry on, gently but *persistently*.

"How do I do that?" you ask. "What happens when I ask for the order and don't get it?" Your natural curiosity should compel you to ask the prospect why she hesitates to place the order at that time. And as the prospect tells you, you might now actually get the real or final obstacle in your path, to learn what else you have to do to get the business.

Once you have identified this objection, answer it as you would any objection—with one exception. This time ask, "Assuming I can take care of that concern for you, is there anything else keeping you from buying now?" If there is, you'll hear it at this point. Once you have uncovered the real reason for resistance and dealt with it, you are home with a sale. Test this approach, and again gently resist taking no for an answer. You will find your sales increasing.

Set Up a Later Contact

What if, in the end, you finally don't get the sale? Before hanging up, draw on that sales axiom that says you should always exit with an opportunity to re-enter. If you are working in other than the one-call-to-close situation, develop a strategy to set up the opportunity to call back at a later time. This can take the form of a soft offer: "Mr. Brandt, I appreciate your time in talking with me about your situation. I am going to take the liberty of adding you to my mailing list to ensure that you are kept informed of new product developments here. When we offer a product more suitable to your needs, I will get back in touch with you." Or you can choose a more forceful course of action by stating, "I am going to send you some additional literature and a letter with some further thoughts for you to keep in mind. I will call you in two weeks to be sure you got the information and see what your feelings are then."

Often the situation itself will dictate the wording of your reentry route. The prospect may have spelled out a budget cycle beyond his control or hinted at some internal changes that make it natural for you to suggest a call back. If you are dealing with individual consumers, you might merely say you will keep in touch, and make a note to give that prospect a call back after a set period of time—say three months. Put these names in a prospect file if you think they are viable possibilities for such follow-up, and get back to them when promised. Finally, your situation may change, with added new products, restructured prices, or something else to make your offer more attractive for converting those marginal prospects into customers.

Wrapping Up the Call

On the brighter side, if the call went exceptionally well and you close the sale, use the opportunity to ask for referrals. Say, "Oh, by the way, whom can you recommend who might be interested in my products? I get a lot of business from referrals." Assure the prospect or new customer that you will keep the referral confidential if they so desire.

And congratulations are in order. Following your carefully thought-out call strategy, you have gotten that all-important order. You have made the sale. But don't talk yourself out of it. Immediately, your goal becomes to wrap up the call and hang up.

After closing a sale, you experience a sense of both relief and exhilaration. Relief comes from the natural nervousness you felt and in response to your continuing professional desire to do well at your job. Exhilaration should come from realizing you have been successful and are one step closer to (or beyond) your goal. You may be tempted to chat a while longer. *Don't do it*! You are giving your customer time to change her mind. Even more damaging, you may say something off the cuff that causes her to rethink her decision. You want to speedily yet politely conclude the interview and get on to your next sale. You should have a thought-out concluding statement that shows your appreciation for her business. Don't forget to say thank you. Perhaps go on to point out that you are confident that this is the beginning of a long and mutually beneficial relationship. Use the exhilaration you feel after a sale to close the next one.

ON YOUR OWN

1. Return one more time to the prospect you used to complete this activity in Chapters 6, 7, and 8. Which closing technique do you think might work best in the situation you've been developing?

2. Using the closing technique you selected, develop a closing statement or series of statements to use in the call. Record it into a tape recorder (or ask a friend or co-worker to hear you out), play it back, and evaluate how you sounded. What would you change?

3. *Special Assignment*: At this point, you have planned and prepared for a full teleselling call. Pick up the telephone now and call the individual consumer or business you've been practicing with from Chapter 6. Conduct a full teleselling interview. Then evaluate your results.

		Yes	No
SELF-INVENTORY	1. I keep in mind from the opening "Hello" that I will have to ask for the order.	____	____
	2. I recognize asking for the order as a natural conclusion to the sales interview.	____	____
	3. I am alert for buying signals from the prospect.	____	____
	4. I use a buying signal as an opportunity to try to close the sale.	____	____
	5. I ask the prospect for the order as often as is necessary to get the business.	____	____

10 Apply

THE KEY

Your interaction with the prospect-turned-customer does not end with the closed sale. There are steps you need to take upon closing the sale to insure that the now-customer has a smooth and positive initial experience with you and your company. Also, because customers are expensive to secure and are the most likely source of future sales, you want to build a solid and lasting relationship with them. Finally, you want to be sure that they receive prompt and courteous attention. This chapter addresses these three areas of concern—service after the sale, building long-term satisfaction, and handling customer follow-up calls—to enable you to employ that sixth "A" in the Straight A's of teleselling: Apply service.

APPLY SERVICE AFTER THE SALE

Many salespeople who are good at persuading prospects to act nonetheless find their careers in jeopardy because they think their work is done when a sale is closed. What these salespeople fail to realize is that the customer is not finished once a purchase decision is made. Because the customer has more to lose with a problematic purchase than does the salesperson who made the sale, the customer constantly evaluates the performance of the products purchased and the companies behind them. The successful teleseller knows this and develops a service-after-the-sale procedure that assures both immediate and long-term customer satisfaction.

As soon as you complete a call, you should wrap up the paperwork and follow-up procedures. If you made a sale, get the orders off your desk and into the right hands for processing to ensure that the customer has a smooth and flawless experience with your company. That way he will probably stay a customer *and* will also refer friends, relatives, neighbors, or colleagues to your company and you.

List what procedures you must follow to completely and successfully wrap up a sale:

1. _____

2. _____

3. _____

4. _____

5. _____

One key to wrapping up a call is maintaining good organization. An organized wrap-up takes a minimum of your time now and saves you time in the future. And completing the details of the sale you just made lets you concentrate better on the next call you handle. Does your list include completing paperwork—updating records, noting results in your call or customer log, completing and forwarding the details of an order, making a note to call a referral, and the like? How about clearing your desk of materials (files, forms, product sheets) used during the call? Don't carry work from one call over into the handling of the next.

You might want to put the list you've just developed on a card and keep it handy for review. Use it to check your work and to remind you of what you have to do to completely finish one call before going on to the next.

Your customer has not seen you, does not know about your surroundings, has not even seen your product yet. This increases the emphasis you must place on applying service. One way to address this problem is to mail something in follow-up. It might be a confirmation of what you and the customer agreed to or a summary of the details of fulfillment, all, of course, accompanied by a "thank you" for the order. This activity also begins your transition from teleseller to relationship partner. To make your mailing effective:

1. Use business cards that feature your photograph. This makes you more than a voice on a telephone (or worse, on voice mail) and personalizes your business relationship.

2. Customize any form letter you send, or develop a data bank of standard paragraphs upon which you can draw to assemble a customized letter. In all cases, print or type the letter. Don't just send a photocopy of a form letter.

3. Make sure that what you send has a neat and professional look. You may not have (or need) four-color full-bleed brochures on heavy stock that are tucked into customized envelopes, but even a simple letter accompanied by an information sheet says something about you and your business. With word processing, page layout, and laser printing services available from your nearest photocopy center, unattractive pieces of mail are simply no longer acceptable.

4. Put your material(s) in the mail immediately. This demonstrates your business professionalism, your desire to be of service, and your prompt reliability.

5. If your mailing sets up a follow-up call, the call should occur not sooner than three days (to allow the mail to get there) nor later than five days (so what you sent isn't forgotten) after your communication goes in the mail.

Finally, applying service offers you several opportunities to better satisfy the needs of both you and your customer through:

- *Cross-selling related products.* Sell the father who just ordered new winter clothes for his children something from your new line of insulated boots, or sell the office manager who just ordered supplies for a new filing system extra cases of copier paper. Cross-selling not only increases customer satisfaction by insuring the best possible use of his initial purchase, but it increases your per-call sales and revenue as well.

- *Maintaining between-orders contact.* Occasionally check with the customer to be sure she continues to be satisfied with your product or to learn of any changes at the customer site that might offer you additional selling opportunities.

- *Resupplying.* If your product requires supplies, the telephone enables

. you to quickly and easily ensure that the needed supplies arrive at the appropriate time.

The net result of any or all of these activities is increased customer loyalty. You become the one on whom customers rely to help them out. You become the one customers praise when talking with their colleagues about vendors. You become the one your competitors envy because, when they call, they run into *your* record of outstanding service as an objection.

A final goal of applying service in your call strategy is to set up the next call. It is axiomatic in selling that a buyer does not contact the seller unless something is wrong. It is for you to arrange the next contact. This keeps you in control of the relationship, assures a smooth continuation of business, and reassures the customer of your sincere interest in his satisfaction with your product. But don't be a pest. Let business or product-related circumstances dictate your follow-up-call cycle. For example, as you increase your product knowledge, you can renew excitement for your product among your customers by pointing out that they may be underutilizing it and showing them how to get even greater gains from their purchase. You might be able to offer product enhancements—new add-ons or new uses for existing optional items—that will extend the useful life of your products. The beauty of teleselling is that you merely need to pick up the telephone, place the call, and deliver meaningful postcall customer service.

APPLY SERVICE TO BUILD LONG-TERM RELATIONSHIPS

The goal of many selling organizations today is to build long-term relationships with their customers. This assures customer satisfaction and repeat business and also creates a mechanism for addressing problems before they become business-threatening. Relationship building can be as easily and effectively accomplished by telesellers as by face-to-face salespeople.

People who do not sell for a living speculate that they would be good at teleselling because they like people (who doesn't?) or because they like to help people (public service would make a better career). The true sales professional takes this thinking one step further: She has a genuine concern for people and for helping them solve their problems. Such a person takes a proactive rather than a reactive approach to applying service, converting her concern to action before being told to do so. If you enjoy converting caring into action, applying service and building lasting relationships will come to you naturally.

To apply proactive customer service:

- Anticipate and address the needs of the customer before the customer calls them to your attention.

- Approach your service activities in a positive manner.

- Assure that the customer gains maximum benefit from your company's products.

- Look for opportunities that allow the customer to benefit from greater use of your company's products.

- Take the actions appropriate to resolve any conflicts or difficulties as soon as you learn of their existence.

Knowing Customers

A necessary prerequisite, of course, is to know your customers. Take the following test. It will make you aware of what you need to know to apply proactive service, test your knowledge of your best customers, and identify any weaknesses in your approach to knowing and serving your customers. Begin by selecting the top five accounts for which you are responsible. From memory, using customer files or other information only as a last resort, score yourself on statements 1 through 9. Decide on your score by using Scale A for statements 1 through 8 and Scale B for statement 9. Record each score in the appropriate box in Table 10.1.

1. I know the name and title of the key contact at this account.
2. This key contact knows me.
3. I know the name of a backup contact.
4. This backup contact knows me.
5. I know which of my products this customer buys.
6. I know how often this customer buys products from me.
7. I know which of my products are crucial to this customer's business/operations.

8. I know which of my competitors' products this customer uses.

9. I have spoken with this customer's key contact.

If you support an outside sales operation or if your company sells through an authorized distributor network, add statement 10. Use Scale A to score.

10. I know the name of this customer's sales or dealer representative.

SCALE A

5—I know that for sure.
4—I think I know that, but give me a minute.
3—I could come close on this one.
2—I'm not sure. Let me look it up.
1—Boy, I just don't know.

SCALE B

(*Note*: Alter the time span as appropriate to your markets and products.)
5—At least once in the past 3 months.
4—At least once in the past 6 months.
3—At least once in the past 9 months.
2—At least once in the past 12 months.
1—I've never talked with the contact.

TABLE 10.1. HOW WELL DO I KNOW MY CUSTOMERS?

Customer	1	2	3	4	5	6	7	8	9	10	TOTAL
1											
2											
3											
4											
5											
TOTAL											

Total your columns both across and down. If your TOTAL in the lower right box equals or exceeds 200, you already apply excellent long-term customer service. If you scored between 150 and 199 points, you are on the right track but need to pay greater attention to certain areas (*Hint*: look at those columns where 2s and 3s predominate for suggestions on where to improve). If you have between 100 and 149 points, you should pay greater attention to the application-of-service aspect of your teleselling work. If you have fewer than 100 points, we can only hope you are new to teleselling or are in a one-call-to-close situation.

Building Relationships

Long-term relationships between customer and seller are characterized by mutual trust, open and honest communication, and the goal of reciprocating prosperity. There are several actions you can take to build such relationships with your customers:

1. *Get the initial order right.*   Take extra care to ensure you do your paperwork right, follow up within your company to guarantee timely fulfillment, and notify the customer immediately if something goes wrong— the promised delivery date slips, the color requested is temporarily out-of-stock, or the like.

2. *Contact the new customer early and at appropriate intervals to ensure that everything is satisfactory.*   Such occasions might be when delivery is scheduled, when installation has been completed and when you suspect a refill of supplies is in order. Such calls reinforce in the mind of the customer that you are interested in his problems, needs, and concerns, as well as in present opportunities to secure repeat business.

3. *Establish a diary to guarantee regular contact with all assigned customers.*   Prioritize your accounts in order of their importance to you and your importance to them—using the volume of business they do with you, the frequency of their orders, or similar criteria—and contact each as the need and circumstances dictate.

4. *Remain an informed and involved teleseller.*   Be involved in your company, your industry, your market, and your customers' lives. Take an active interest in what you sell, who buys it, and how it is used. Share your continually expanding knowledge with your customers and co-workers. Make a difference.

The success of your business depends as much on providing good service as it does on achieving great sales results. Begin, on your first call, to apply service to all the customers you acquire.

APPLY SERVICE TO YOUR CUSTOMER RESPONSES

It is a sad comment on today's telephone practices that consumers generally regard telesellers as rude, indifferent, insensitive, unthinking verbal robots. The only good news in such a finding is that, if you discipline yourself to handle the various telephone situations you encounter in a sound, customer-oriented manner, you can have a memorable and favorable impact on the people whom you contact. That impact will transcend the call itself, serving not only you and your work, but also your company.

Incoming Calls

A primary assumption made about you while creating this book is that you are an outbound teleseller, one who initiates contact with prospective customers. On the other hand, in the day-to-day operation of a business, perhaps you are the recipient of as many calls as you make. With that in mind, the following suggestions apply to handling incoming calls in a manner that inspires trust, confidence, and a favorable outcome.

- *Answer the telephone promptly.* The recommended practice is within two or three rings. This shows that you are not just sitting waiting for the phone to ring but are not too busy to take an interest in the caller.

- *Shrug your shoulders and smile.* This mental and physical break from whatever you are doing when the telephone rings prepares you to give the caller your undivided attention.

- *Identify yourself and your company.* It is simple courtesy, and it ensures you won't waste time on a call not intended for you or your company.

- *Give the caller your full name.* You avoid the caller having to ask for your name, and, when dealing with an irate caller, you disarm her with your openness and willingness to be of service.

- *Avoid impatience.* Let the other party believe that talking to him is the most important thing you have to deal with at this time.

- *Learn and use the caller's name.* And, unless or until otherwise instructed, use a title (Mr., Ms., Dr., or the like) and the last name.

- *Speak directly into the mouthpiece.* This ensures you are heard, helps block out background sound, and lets you better project your voice.

- *Match your talk speed to that of the caller.* This is one of the adaptive techniques you'll develop in Chapter 11.

- *Don't interrupt unless it's absolutely necessary.* The more you hear, the more you learn about the caller and the situation. Most people will give you more information than you would ask for.

- *If appropriate, find the requested party as soon as possible.* If the call isn't for you, transfer the call in a prompt and professional manner (see "Taking a Message" on page 124).

- *Think "courtesy" in your choice of words.* Adding *thank you,* or *please,* or other words that seek or encourage cooperation serves you well in all calls.

- *Sound (and be) interested in the caller.* Pay attention, ask questions, listen, rephrase, and in other ways show you are there to be of service.

- *Don't pass the buck.* Regardless of who or what caused the situation or problem, in the mind of the person to whom you are talking, you are the company. Think of your firm as a one-person entrepreneurship. The caller does.

- *Be prepared to take accurate messages.* Practice the steps provided below (see "Taking a Message" on page 124).

- *Let the caller hang up first.* Without getting into a waiting game, after you have wrapped up the call and exchanged good-byes, let the caller disconnect the call.

Complaint Calls

The complaint call is not fun to handle. But before getting to techniques for handling one effectively, a word of caution: Many calls tellesellers label as "irate" are induced by the behavior of the telleseller handling the call. To avoid inducing an irate call yourself, remember and practice courteous communication techniques. Don't get into an argument with your prospects and customers. To keep a cool head, stick to the facts and remain objective about what you are presenting. Finally, remember something all salespeople know about that other tough circumstance, rejection: Don't take it personally. Customer anger isn't directed at you (unless you've induced it by your conduct) but at the situation. You will only make things worse if you lose control of your own emotions.

Handle the complaint call with these additional tactics:

- *Respond to the caller on a personal level.*   Drop canned responses you may be tempted to use. With the complaining or irate caller, more than with any other caller you handle, employ sincerity, empathy, and sympathy. You can act in your "official" capacity later, but first bring the caller under control.

- *Make the caller feel she is right.*   Let her ventilate her frustration. If you or your company is in the wrong, admit it. Acknowledge that you see there is a problem that needs attention. Then listen and gather information to use when it is your turn to talk.

- *Restate the problem to make sure you understand it.*   Be sure you and the customer agree on what the problem is before proceeding to solve it.

- *Get the details you'll need.*   Go back to the beginning, ask questions, and collect the information you need to act. In this way you will better manage the caller *and* defuse the emotion of the situation. You are also demonstrating your interest and concern.

- *Use encouraging words and phrases, such as "I understand how that can make you angry" or "You were right to call about this."*   You can disarm and appease an angry caller in this way. However, don't make commitments until you know all the facts and are sure the commitment you are going to make is within your authority and can be carried out. Otherwise you'll have a more irate caller the next time.

- *Never interrupt.*   Not a good practice at any time, interrupting an angry caller is to be absolutely avoided.

- *Don't duplicate the caller's talk speed.*   Employ a moderate, even, calm tone to your voice.

- *Speak authoritatively when you do speak, asserting yourself and your control into the call.*   You are the expert and the one to solve the complaint. With words and voice, show that you know what you are doing and that you will do what has to be done to satisfy the caller.

- *Apologize for the company.* Assure the caller that what happened is not what was intended. Make it clear that both you and the company are sorry, and then proceed to solutions.

- *Ask what can be done to correct the problem to the customer's satisfaction.* Make sure you understand both what the caller wants done and what can be done. Reconcile any differences between these two approaches, make clear what you intend to do, and ask for agreement that the approach you plan will be satisfactory. Don't leave the subject until you have that agreement.

- *Compromise where you can.* When you see the opportunity, respond, "Maybe we don't have all the facts. Let me call fulfillment." Such a demonstration of flexibility will establish good faith and show you are listening with interest.

- *Don't make excuses.* What happened in the past is over. You want to get on with the future and with solving the situation to the customer's satisfaction.

- *Take action.* That's what the caller wants. Almost any positive action will do. Fix what you can or what you have the authority to correct. Explain, if you cannot fix the situation yourself, who will take the final and definitive action needed to set the matter straight.

- *Follow up and call back.* Do what you say you will, then call back to be sure the customer is satisfied. Be ready, if the matter is not entirely resolved, to provide a status check on where matters stand.

Taking a Message

Frequently, you answer the telephone and the call is for someone else. If this happens or if the call is about something you cannot handle, your first option is to transfer the call as effortlessly as possible. If you know who is to handle the call, say to whom you'll transfer, for example, "Mr. Martin in accounting will handle your question. I'll transfer you to him now at extension 23." In that way, if you are unsuccessful, the other party knows whom to call back and where to reach him. Be sure to avoid the casual "Hold on a second, I'll get someone."

If you don't know who should handle the call, it's up to you to find out. Before you begin the search, ask (don't tell) the other party to hold or offer to have the call returned later. When you have located the correct person to handle the call, tell that person who is calling and what the call is about. That will save the caller repeating the problem.

If you can't locate the person for whom the call was intended or the person who should handle the call, you will have to take a message. To do that flawlessly, follow these steps:

- *Take responsibility for messages.* Every call has a message or it wouldn't have been placed. When you pick up the telephone, be ready to take a message.

- *Have a message pad and pencil within easy reach.* Use the company message pad or clean, plain paper—something you can leave with the message recipient that is clear and understandable by itself.

- *Identify yourself and ask if you can help; for example, "I'm Joann Jackson. I work with Mr. Martin. Can I help you?"* Perhaps you can save all parties some time by answering a brief question, providing a needed detail, or otherwise handling the caller's needs without further ado.

- *Always offer to take a message.* If you can't help, state your intention to see that a message gets to the right person: "I'll take a message for you and see that Mr. Martin gets it."

- *Ask for an explanation of any details that you do not understand.* After the caller has provided you with the details, repeat them back to ensure you got it down correctly.

- *Complete a message form even if there is no message.* At least write the time of the call and get the name of the person who called. If the caller won't provide that, leave a note that a person (man or woman) called and wouldn't leave a message or said he or she would call back. The intended recipient may know who called or what the call was about from the brief clues that even such a short message contains.

Message-taking techniques wouldn't be complete without an established procedure for seeing to it that the messages are routed to the intended recipient. This is especially important when an office has people working in the field who, thus, are not in every day. The steps are simple:

1. Field people should have a set call-in time for picking up messages—not precisely 4:27 P.M. every day, but an established range to allow for circumstances, say after 3 P.M. or before 10 A.M.

2. Those taking messages should make the caller aware of the message-pick-up practice and ask when after the established call-in time it would be convenient to receive a call back. If the caller doesn't understand the callback process, he is left wondering when the return call will come. Given that the call is unique and important to the person who places it, it isn't hard to imagine him expecting to hear from someone within the hour. If the return is made in accordance with established procedures but not until the next day, the person returning the call may have an irate situation on her hands.

3. All messages should note the requested callback time.

4. All calls with a requested callback should be returned. Even when no new information is available, show businesslike courtesy and maintain good customer relations with a returned call.

Returning Calls

When someone takes a message for you, an obligation is created. In the mind of a caller who leaves a message, you are going to call back, and soon. In fact, if the caller is not acquainted with your callback procedures or if you don't follow them after the caller becomes acquainted with them, you can expect an icy if not hostile reaction when you don't call back within the hour. The obligation to return calls is critically important to maintaining a positive environment with your prospects and customers, one conducive to doing business. Resolve now to return your calls promptly. Here are some tips to help you:

*   *Establish a procedure that you can follow.*   All calls should be returned as quickly as possible. Depending on your routine, plan now for the time of day when you will handle callbacks.

*   *Plan to return your calls immediately unless a message indicates a specific time for a callback.*

*   *Stick to your plan.*   Discipline yourself to start your plan today. Get off to a good start, then keep at it.

*   *Make the easy calls first.*   Some messages inspire creative excuses for

why you can't return the call immediately, especially if the call will involve an unpleasant report, action, or outcome. To overcome this, sort your messages according to their level of difficulty, complexity, or the like. Then start with the easiest-to-handle return calls first. You get "in the swing of things" and have accomplished a great deal already before you get to the ones more difficult to handle.

- *Gather the materials you will need before beginning your callback session.*   Whether it's a file, correspondence, forms, or just a note pad, having it first will make the calls go more smoothly and more quickly, and with improved results.

- *Return your calls immediately.*   It bears repeating: Don't put off returning calls. Prompt callbacks ensure that none of your callers become irate, help keep your work load manageable, minimize the chances of a backlog growing from unattended business, inspire trust and confidence, and find the original purpose of the call still fresh in the mind of the caller.

Following these suggestions will put you in control of your relationship with your customers. And, as that control leads to more and more long-term relationships with your customers, you will see your teleselling results steadily improving.

ON YOUR OWN

1. Assume that the customer you've been using in Chapters 6 through 9 has made the purchase you advocated. What did the customer order?

2. Itemize the paperwork and other immediate postcall follow-up you will have to do to ensure the customer receives what was ordered when it was promised.

3. Outline a strategy to develop a long-term relationship with this customer.

		Yes	No
SELF-INVENTORY	1. I systematically complete all paperwork necessary as a wrap-up to my calls as soon as each call ends.	____	____

2. I keep in touch with my accounts on a schedule that reflects their need for and use of my products. ____ ____

3. I can identify at least two key contacts at each one of my accounts. ____ ____

4. My customers know me and the products I represent. ____ ____

5. Before putting the file away after a customer contact, I enter the next scheduled contact in my diary. ____ ____

11 Adapt

THE KEY

If your interaction with the prospect involves more than a one-call close or if you are exclusively a customer-service teleseller, you might want to add yet another "A" to your call strategy. "Adaptive" teleselling calls on you to react not only to the prospect's problems, needs, and concerns, but to her behavior as well. Once you determine the kind of person with whom you are dealing, you adapt your behavior to a style that best enables you to communicate with and influence the prospect in question. This approach to prospects (and customers) has become recognized as an important technique for successful tellesellers. This chapter introduces to you the concept of adaptive selling, provides you with techniques for assessing the social style of individual prospects and customers over the telephone, and then instructs you in how to respond to each one in the most effective manner.

INTERACTING POSITIVELY WITH PEOPLE BY TELEPHONE

Although you might already be a pretty good teleseller, applying adaptive selling techniques to your calls will enable you to become exceptional. You will be more successful at building trust and creating rapport. You will simultaneously save time and achieve your call objectives. By altering the way you communicate and interact with people over the telephone, you will find that your work will be easier, more rewarding, and more enjoyable.

129

Adaptive techniques have as their foundation the observation that, whereas each of us is unique, people exhibit certain qualities and behaviors with enough frequency to make them common. To perhaps demonstrate this, look around your work area at your co-workers. Although everyone is probably wearing clothing appropriate to a work environment, some individuals will be conservatively dressed, others flamboyantly dressed, still others casually dressed, and a final group rather carelessly dressed. Similar differences might occur in their conversational styles, in how they set up the materials they use in their work, and even in what they have for lunch.

These varied yet similar behaviors enable us to identify and categorize the people with whom we are dealing and respond to them in a manner that is both comfortable and effective. Identifying the totality of a person's individual qualities—known as one's social style—as compared to the similar qualities of others lets you place a prospect in a general grouping of people with like (not identical) behavior. For our purposes, four such groupings are sufficient (the original researchers who developed the concept of assessing personalities and responding appropriately identified eighty-one groupings, far too many for us to worry about in the few minutes we spend with each person on the telephone).

Once you have successfully identify the social style of a person with whom you are dealing, you adapt your behavior as best you can to parallel that style. Adapting to the prospect's or customer's social style increases the likelihood that you'll interact in the positive manner called for to fulfill needs and satisfy desires. *Adaptive selling*, then, is a process by which you identify and then reflect the personal qualities of the other person.

There are certain problems associated with trying to assess social styles by telephone. You cannot pick up on some of the signals you would get in a face-to-face encounter—clothing, interactions with others, and lifestyle details such as furniture, decoration, and setting. Further, because telephone custom calls for contacts to be brief, certainly more brief than in-person contact, you gather fewer clues in the short time such interactions take place. That, in turn, limits the depth to which you can go to assess individual social styles.

To review, one's social style is described as distinctive individual qualities and behaviors considered as a whole. Frequent or common qualities and behaviors can be grouped. These grouped qualities or behaviors among people occur with enough frequency to justify developing techniques for dealing with them. You can learn to recognize and respond to the qualities and behaviors in an appropriate manner. Your goal in this exercise is to create a positive interaction that achieves your objectives while fulfilling the prospect's or customer's needs and desires.

Three precautions are in order before you apply the techniques recommended here. You are not becoming a psychologist or therapist. You are merely becoming acquainted with the various social styles you will encounter in your work. You want to be sensitive and responsive to them for the obvious reason that it helps you get your work done.

Further, adaptive teleselling is not intended as a means of passing judgment on any one social style in preference to another. To a teleseller, an intimidating or dominating person is no better or worse than someone who is calm and supportive. On the job, you have to deal effectively with both.

Finally, you are not expected to be a chameleon, magically changing into a different creature with each call you handle. Rather, within the bounds of your own personality, attitudes, and prejudices, you want to work to create the positive interaction that a well-executed adaptive-call-handling strategy can provide.

How do you detect the clues to a person's social style? It's almost too obvious and simple: You listen. You listen to what is said and how it is said. The other clues to one's social style include:

1. The speed and pacing of a person's speech.

2. The tone of voice used.

3. The rate at which a person thinks.

4. The quickness with which conclusions are reached and decisions made.

5. The words and phrases used and what they mean.

You employ all of these signals to help you place your prospects into one of four social styles: Driven-Dominant, Expressive-Extroverted, Amiable-Sociable, and Analytical-Technical.

THE FOUR SOCIAL STYLES

Recognizing the qualities and behaviors associated with each of the four social styles requires that you evaluate two aspects of a person's behavior: assertiveness and responsiveness. Ranking each of these qualities along a spectrum from 1 to 4 forms the basis of a grid, illustrated in Figure 11.1. The point at which a person's assertiveness (the horizontal component) and responsiveness (the vertical component) intersect identifies the social style to which your prospect belongs.

Assertiveness refers to the efforts each person makes to control the people

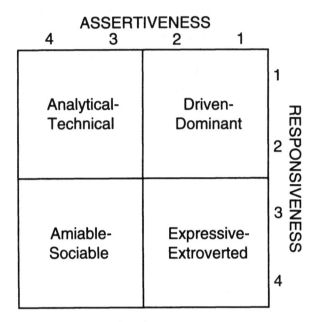

FIGURE 11.1. Charting Social Styles

and things around him, that is, the length to which a person will go to see that his way of thinking or acting is the one that prevails. In Figure 11.1, an assertiveness ranking of 1 describes a person who is highly assertive and, thus, is placed on the extreme right of the scale. Such a person is a risk-taker and will make quick decisions, usually without consulting others. The assertive person is competitive and might try to show off her superior knowledge, perhaps even to intimidate you. Certainly she feels free to interrupt you, especially if you don't speak fast enough. Often serious and humorless, the highly assertive person may strike you as hard-nosed or "all business."

At the other end of the spectrum, a person ranked 4 is low in assertiveness, little concerned with controlling other people or situations. He avoids risks, often relying heavily on data or consensus to minimize the chance of error. Consequently, he makes decisions slowly and is willing, even anxious, to get advice about the best decision to make. Appearing cooperative, a person not seeking to control others is responsive to what others say and sensitive to how they feel about the matter under consideration. Such a person will ask you questions, consider your responses, reach a conclusion, and probably immediately seek approval that it was the right conclusion to reach.

Responsiveness is the effort people make to control themselves and their own emotions in a situation. A responsiveness ranking of 1 describes a person who is highly unresponsive and, thus, makes every attempt to control herself and her emotions in various situations. You will find the unresponsive person to be task oriented, with no great concern for the feelings of others. You would say she is tough-minded, cold, and unemotional about what is being discussed. Described as distant, someone with an unresponsive social style is also characterized as self-disciplined.

A person ranked 4 in responsiveness would exhibit few characteristics of self-control. Having a loose rein on his feelings, the highly responsive person reacts to situations and people emotionally. He wants to be liked and, as a result, will rely on feelings rather than reason in decision making. As one who needs interpersonal relationships, the highly responsive person, exercising limited control over his emotions and feelings, puts a premium on close ties and friendships.

Driven-Dominant

If the intersection of a person's assertiveness and responsiveness rankings occurs somewhere in the upper right quadrant in Figure 11.1, where high assertive and unresponsive qualities prevail, you are dealing with a Driven-Dominant person. Driven-Dominant people work hard to keep their own emotions under control while at the same time attempting to exercise control over you. They expect you to get quickly to the point, handle their questions, and get off the telephone. They are aggressive, sometimes even hostile, and come across as a know-it-all, even as closed-minded.

Demanding and fast talking, the voice of Driven-Dominants might be characterized as loud or harsh or both. They give you little time to think—snapping, for example, "How fast can you get that to me?" or "Just spell it out for me in black and white, will you?"—leading you to perhaps think of them as relentless. To get their way, they might let it be known that they are in some way more experienced than you are at your job: "I know exactly what you're talking about. I used to be a (fill in the blank with your job title here) when I started in this field." Their word choices include "do" or "don't," "should" or "shouldn't," "always" or "never." In other words, they think in extremes. To put you on the defensive immediately, they might respond to your opening comment with, "Yes, what'd you say your name was? Could you spell that?" You might also hear such expressions as, "Get to the point, I don't have time for all these details" or "Give it to me straight." Always aware of time, they will say something like, "I need to get this settled no later than by noon on Friday."

The net effect of the Driven-Dominants' behavior is to simultaneously control you, the situation that brings you and them together, and themselves. They think they are incapable of being wrong (hence, what you consider a risky decision, they see as of little risk) and are unconcerned with what others think. The good news in terms of selling to them is that, if you can accurately mirror their conduct, you will have a quick sale with little or no buyer's remorse.

Expressive-Extroverted

In the lower right quadrant are the Expressive-Extroverted people. While still assertive, Expressive-Extroverted people exercise less control over their own emotions, give them a freer rein. Perhaps image conscious, they are people you'd call Mr. or Ms. Personality, a standout, the life of the party.

Among identifiable Expressive-Extroverted behaviors are a voice that is lively, vibrant, full of feeling, sincere, warm. They have a manner that is relaxed and unhurried and a rate of speech that is uneven as they warm or cool to a subject. The Expressive-Extroverted person is enthusiastic, talks a lot, asks your opinion on things, responds emotionally to situations. They are feeling people, and will say, "That sounds great," "Outstanding," "Wow!" or use other words or expressions that reflect a colorful personality. They might open a call with, "Hi, John, how are you doing today?" Other possible comments include, "I feel we can get this wrapped up, don't you?", and "I think we did the right thing on this, don't you?" and "Isn't it great?" Buying signals coming from an Expressive-Extroverted person might include, "I've given this a lot of thought. What do you think of (the decision)?" or "I really think we made the right choice."

Amiable-Sociable

Amiable-Sociable people, in the lower left quadrant, are less assertive than the Expressive-Extroverted people, yet they are responsive to their own emotions. Amiable-Sociable people are security conscious, which leads to a certain degree of indecisiveness, perhaps allowing for some doubt about what you say. Once the action is agreed on, the Amiable-Sociable person seeks approval from you of the decisions reached.

Amiable-Sociable people have such characteristic behaviors as a nurturing, reassuring, and encouraging voice tone and quality. They will ask a lot of questions as their doubtful-tentative side emerges when it is time to decide or act. Words or phrases such as "I'm not sure" and "It seems like that's the case. What do you think?" and "That could be—I'll have to check; I don't really know" reflect the uncertainty characteristic of the Amiable-Sociable person. You'll also find them to be slow talkers who speak directly into the telephone. You won't have trouble understanding them.

Analytical-Technical

Analytical-Technical people, in the upper left quadrant, are not assertive over others, but they maintain control of their emotions. As a result they tend to be quiet and need to be drawn out in the conversation. Detail oriented, the Analytical-Technical person is concerned with facts, data, the specifics (one way to remain "in control" is to base decisions on reason, not emotion).

In a voice that is calm, flat, unemotional, and paced, Analytical-Technical people will ask who, what, when, where, why, and how. They might respond to something you say with, "I need some specific information" or "Tell me step-by-step exactly what I'm supposed to do." Or they may want to know, "How many days will it take to get this order processed?" An Analytical-Technical person will let you know that, "Without my own workup, I cannot agree to your terms." Other words or phrases include, "the odds are" and "it seems like." Additional clues are the even rate of speech she employs, a general alertness and tendency to respond quickly, and the asking of detailed questions, perhaps more detailed than necessary.

Other verbal clues to the Analytical-Technical person include such questions as "What, precisely, am I to include in what I'm to send you?" and "Can you give me a complete breakdown of what is included in this item (and he will name the item) of your proposal?"

HOW TO ADAPT TO DIFFERENT PERSONAL STYLES

As a professional teleseller, you know that dealing with prospects and customers is more than a matter of chance. Building positive interaction by telephone requires you to respond to others with a behavior, call content, and strategy that compliments their social style. When you are successful, you will inspire confidence and believability while enabling the other party to experience your interest in them. Thus reassured, your prospect's or customer's apprehension, tension, discomfort, or unease, perhaps induced by the call situation, will diminish.

Positive interaction begins when you put yourself in the other party's place, in other words, being empathetic. You know the thoughts that would go through your mind, were you to reverse roles and be on the other end of the line. You'd want to know you can both trust the teleseller and believe the information she is providing. You'd want to be sure your interests are the heart of the conversation, not the selling company's marketing plan. You'd want her to demonstrate and convey a sincere interest in satisfying your needs, desires, and concerns.

You can begin by speaking the prospect's language—not just the words, but how they are delivered, the tone, and the mood behind them. You go a long way in establishing trust and rapport when you sound like the other person, talking like him and using the same words and phrases he does. In effect, you become the other person to the extent possible and within reason. How can the other person help but cooperate with you if you are someone he perceives as really like himself?

Talk at the same rate, with the same tone, inflection, and manner, as the person on the other end of the line. A quick-talking person who speaks in short, perhaps incomplete, sentences will respond positively when you do the same. You subtly establish that you are not just listening, but listening closely. In both manner and words, you are saying you are there to be of service.

Be alert, too, for what the other person's tone of voice says. For example, a flat, low, and unenthusiastic voice, regardless of other social-style clues, might reflect that something is wrong. An expression of concern in such a situation says you are listening to all that is being said and that you are interested in the other person, not yourself. Ask, "Mrs. Adams, I sense something is bothering you. Is there anything I can do to help?"

On the other hand, as the professional in the call, you want to guard against letting your mood show. You may be having one of the worst days in recent memory. If so, you want to begin each call with a shrug, a deep breath, and a smile. Whatever is causing your worsening mood, it isn't the person you're about to call.

Responding to the Driven-Dominant

In the upper right quadrant of the social-styles matrix in Figure 11.1 are the Driven-Dominants. They tend to be direct, impatient, action oriented, and perhaps competitive. Driven-Dominants make quick, definitive decisions. They are not good listeners, as is manifested by the interruptions you experience as they finish your sentences for you. Other interruptions occur as they try to get other things said or done (the prototype Driven-Dominant person will, while talking with you, be working out on an exercycle, shaving with his free hand, and watching the news on TV), reflecting quick thinking as much as poor listening. Fearing change little or not at all, a Driven-Dominant is the most open to your suggestions, as long as they make sense and are presented in the rapid, ticking-off-a-checklist manner characteristic of his style of communicating.

One of the keys to dealing with a person whose style you identify as Driven-Dominant is to get to the point and stick to it. Don't engage in small talk, which you will almost certainly have initiated. Be brief, using short, concise sentences and well-chosen, economical words. Don't challenge her knowledge, but work to add to it, perhaps saying, "I see your point, but maybe you'd also want to consider this information." Let her feel in control. Talk in terms of results and actions, and, when you see the first opportunity, ask for agreement. It is apt to be immediately forthcoming. And when you secure it, move right along, or wrap up and hang up.

Responding to the Expressive-Extroverted

The Expressive-Extroverteds are in the lower right quadrant of Figure 11.1. These people exhibit an open, friendly manner. They possess a high level of self-assurance and confidence and show it, as well as their enthusiasm for everything. Their speech and manner are what you'd call "animated." They like other people and want to be liked by them. This is one of the drives that leads them to ask your opinion on how to proceed, whether with the matter under discussion or with other subjects that may have been brought up. The Expressive-Extroverted person is someone open to new approaches, one who wants the latest. Not concerned with details, he can be responsive to verbal agreements. An emotional person, the Expressive-Extroverted responds with feelings and says so.

Techniques for interacting with Expressive-Extroverted people include trying to get along with them. That is as important as getting a job done or a situation resolved. Confrontation, an either-or or take-it-or-leave-it approach, is out. Also, you're wasting your time trying to pin down facts or details. Instead, let her talk, and rely on your listening skills and other sources (customer files, purchase history, and so on) to learn what you need to know. The Expressive-Extroverted person responds to open-ended questions, telling you more than you wanted to hear. She is prone to ramble off the point, so use questions to bring the discussion back to the subject. Talk about feelings, or in a "feeling" way, yourself. Demonstrate your concern for people. Finally, because she reacts positively to oral agreements, you can accomplish a lot with the Expressive-Extroverted person by telephone.

Responding to the Amiable-Sociable

Amiable-Sociables, in the lower left quadrant of Figure 11.1, are people who characteristically do not assert themselves to others. These people talk readily about their problems and what was done in the face of them. They will seek your reassurance that the matter was handled in the right way. This deliberative decision-making process, backed with a dose of self-second-guessing, presents you with a person who will resist sudden or significant change. The Amiable-Sociable person might strike you as disorganized and slow and thoughtful about decisions. As a defense against quick decisions, he tends to ask a lot of questions. These may be general questions about your product or about you and the company or specific questions about details of the purchase, delivery schedule, follow-up services, and the like.

To deal effectively with an Amiable-Sociable person, you will have to call heavily on your skills as a communicator. You have to be more patient than you would be with an assertive person, and you have to work to persuade an Amiable-Sociable person to act. She requires you to quickly evolve a call structure, carefully choosing what you'll say and then sticking to your plan, proceeding very deliberately through your call strategy. Back up what you say with proof. Be sure to stick to the point, not rambling off the subject, even if the other person initiates the wandering. Amiable-Sociables don't like surprises, preferring to see how things fit into an already existing pattern. For you to manage this mind-set, you are to take a thoughtful, methodical approach to the call, its content, and strategy.

To get agreement with Amiable-Sociables, stress security and the reliability of the company or the course of action you recommend. When advocating your product, go over the benefits of your recommendation precisely, covering what you perceive as key concerns of the other party in a point-by-point fashion. Ask the prospect for agreement, and, if he hesitates, quickly reinforce your points and ask again. You might even have to force a decision, presenting either-or alternatives that would offend an Expressive-Extroverted person.

Responding to the Analytical-Technical

Finally, in the upper left quadrant of Figure 11.1 are the Analytical-Technical people, those who don't assert themselves over others, but make a strong effort to control themselves. They react to you and what you say in the slowest, most thoughtful and deliberate manner of all the people you encounter. Analytical-Technical people, who like facts and figures and see information as a means to controlling their decision-making process, ask knowledgeable questions and give you precise details. If you were to ask an Analytical-Technical person, "Where do our truckers exit Interstate 80 to make the delivery?" he or she would first ask, "Are you coming east or west?" and then respond, "Look for the Stocker-Bellefonte exit. It's Exit #147, just west of mile marker 181. At the bottom of the hill..." (An Expressive-Extroverted person, on the other hand, might say, "The next exit past Danville," without knowing whether your driver was going to pass Danville.) The Analytical-Technical person will keep up with you word for word and follow your instructions, usually to the letter. You can tell because it is being written down exactly, with pauses to ask a question if something is missed or found unclear. Analytical-Technical people are detail oriented and well organized, and, when they act, it is usually decisively, perhaps after a little deliberation.

To deal with Analytical-Technicals, you have to be as analytical and technical as they are. If you aren't an Analytical-Technical yourself, this is perhaps the hardest person to adapt to. You'll have to do your best. You must be specific if you are going to succeed at getting an agreement. You are on safe ground if you stick to facts, details, data. Give as detailed a presentation of your points as you can, making solid, factual statements: "Based on the figures you've given me, I recommend 500 of our Model 221C shipped to arrive on Friday," not "I've got an idea of what you'll need. It'll go out next week." The Analytical-Technical person is also put off by disorganization. Bluffing (which you'll usually couch in general terms anyway) can be harmful. And such a person responds unfavorably if you employ a pushy or aggressive style.

Early in a call, the Analytical-Technical person may suggest to an insurance teleseller, "I'll give you my present coverages, and you tell me if you can duplicate it." He will proceed, quoting all coverages and riders supplied with the policy being discussed. And you should respond in exactly the manner asked. Take notes, answer back in exactly the order presented, and elaborate where needed in a direct, specific manner. Review the meaning of your coverages, show how they apply, explain the exceptions, tell what you can do about them, and wrap up by asking if everything is clear. You passed the test if there is first silence, and then "Yes."

When you successfully assess and respond to an individual's social style and then work to achieve your call goal(s) via positive interaction with the style encountered, you are using one of the most sophisticated, powerful teleselling tools available. If your products are comprehensive and competitive, if you learn and address the needs that grow out of the prospect's situation, if you consider and react to each prospect's social style, and if you interact in a positive manner with each prospect, you can achieve a greater level of success in teleselling.

ON YOUR OWN

1. Create six copies of the social-styles matrix illustrated in Figure 11.1.

2. Over the telephone, engage six people who are informed enough to carry on such a conversation (customers, co-workers, family members, friends, etc.) in a discussion of how they make use of the product you are teleselling.

3. Identify which of the four social styles applies to each person you interview. Note the clues you detected that led to your decision. Perhaps, if the situation permits, you can describe what you've just done and ask each interviewee if he or she agrees with your social-style assessment.

	Yes	No
SELF-INVENTORY 1. I recognize the need to manage the course and direction of each call I handle.	____	____
2. I treat each person with whom I talk as a unique individual.	____	____
3. I behave toward people in the manner that responds to their social style.	____	____
4. I induce a favorable reaction to myself and my recommendations for action in the calls I handle.	____	____
5. I distinguish among the individual behaviors and qualities of my prospects and place each in the appropriate adaptive category.	____	____

12

Trouble-Free Telecommunication

THE KEY

Good communication skills are the mark of anyone who sells for a living. Restricting your selling exclusively to the telephone poses some unique communication challenges and opportunities, for your entire productivity rests so heavily on your ability to communicate. You must give attention to eradicating the physical, verbal, and mental obstacles you may have to being a good communicator. You must make use of just the right words as you approach your prospect, advocate your products, and answer objections. You must work to develop a good selling voice, one that is clear and audible, its tone and volume well controlled. This chapter will show you how to build and maintain clear channels of communication with your prospects and customers, how to recognize and use good selling words, and how to determine the strengths and weaknesses of your voice as well as how to work on improving it.

BUILDING OBSTACLE-FREE COMMUNICATION

Have you listened to yourself on the telephone lately? You might benefit from placing a tape recorder next to your telephone and recording an hour of the calls you handle. Replay the tape. Do you make non-word noises, saying "Well, uh, Mr. Dell, um, ah, I think, er . . ."? Do you misplace things

141

and have to put your prospects and customers on hold while you look for them? Do prospects and customers frequently respond to the things you say by asking, "I'm not sure I understand what you mean. Can you run that by me again?" Answering yes indicates symptoms of poor communication on your part.

Communication Barriers

Those are but a few examples of the numerous barriers to effective communication that can exist. The barriers can be grouped into four categories to help gain an understanding of them and facilitate correction or improvement.

1. *Mental barriers.*   You might be *nervous* when you feel you have to persuade a prospect to accept a lesser product because you know the preferred model is too expensive. You might be *defensive* at having to notify the customer that the delivery date for her order has slipped by two weeks. You could be in a *poor frame of mind*, either from work- or non-work-related circumstances. You might be *worried* about an earlier call that didn't go well or about your upcoming performance evaluation.

    These and numerous other events, situations, and thoughts serve to distract you. They prevent concentration on what you are supposed to be doing: seeking prospects and closing sales. You are unable to manage the call to the goals you might otherwise have instinctively mastered. You cannot address problems you are ready, able, and authorized to solve.

2. *Personal barriers.*   Your level of enthusiasm and the state of your positive mental attitude are examples of personal barriers. Do you believe in the value of your product and appreciate your vital role in the industry you serve? Do you see your company and its products as important elements in the lives of your customers? Do you appreciate the importance of your selling work to all parties involved: your customer, your company, your community, and you? If you responded yes to most or all of these, do you show the resulting enthusiasm and positive mental boost? If not, can you simulate them? At the same time, can you identify the reasons why you aren't enthusiastic and then work to overcome them?

    Your ability to communicate, your knowledge of your products, and your skills at persuasion all contribute to how well you establish your attitude and generate enthusiasm. Are you confident that things are going to work out, that you are going to succeed in your work, that you are going to successfully handle both difficult and easy calls, and that you are in command of the information needed to answer questions or objections? When you have the data and other information you need, can you advocate your recommendations in a clear, straightforward, businesslike manner? Are you a logical and organized thinker? Does your presentation reflect these facts?

3. *Verbal barriers.*   Your verbal mannerisms can bar effective communication. Do your prospects and customers understand you? Do you talk too fast or too slow? Do you speak clearly, or do you mumble? Do the words you use provide clear, positive, believable images? Even speaking mannerisms over which you have little control, such as possessing a local dialect, can pose sometimes serious problems for you as you try to communicate with others.

4. *Physical barriers.*   Are you and your work station ready for you to handle your calls? Do you have everything you need at hand: files, forms, product literature, equipment? Are there distractions around you: incomplete paperwork from a previous call, for example, or coffee and crumbs from an earlier snack? Do other people interrupt you? If you are not ready to handle your calls, you can expect that things will go wrong. You won't be at your best, and the management of your calls will elude you.

Overcoming Communication Barriers

People evaluate you on the basis of the interest you show in their needs, desires, and concerns; the quality of the information you deliver; and your speech, politeness, and appearance. All of these things are measured by your prospects on the basis of how well you communicate (send and receive) with them by telephone.

With the tape you made earlier of your side of several calls, use the following checklist of desirable communication attributes to evaluate your skill at communicating by telephone. After listening to yourself, circle the number from 1 to 10 (10 being the best possible score) that best indicates your performance on each attribute. You might ask a colleague for a similar rating to see if your self-evaluation is on the mark.

1.	Enthusiasm	1	2	3	4	5	6	7	8	9	10
2.	Naturalness	1	2	3	4	5	6	7	8	9	10
3.	Concentration	1	2	3	4	5	6	7	8	9	10
4.	Interest	1	2	3	4	5	6	7	8	9	10
5.	Pacing	1	2	3	4	5	6	7	8	9	10
6.	Knowledgeability	1	2	3	4	5	6	7	8	9	10
7.	Detected motion	1	2	3	4	5	6	7	8	9	10
8.	Spontaneity	1	2	3	4	5	6	7	8	9	10
9.	Volume	1	2	3	4	5	6	7	8	9	10
10.	Distracting sounds	1	2	3	4	5	6	7	8	9	10

Your ability to communicate and the success with which you manage the calls you handle are closely related. To overcome call behaviors that you have identified as adversely affecting your communication, concentrate on what you are doing. Concentration, combined with a positive mental attitude and an inherent expectation that you will achieve your goals and manage your calls well, will enable you to influence both the thinking and the behavior of the other party as well as the outcome of the call. That makes it appropriate to work to overcome mental barriers.

A champion skier, standing atop a run that looks like Niagara Falls and realizing that she is about to hurtle off the end of it at speeds in excess of 150 miles an hour, knows that talking or thinking about staying in control is one thing. Doing it is another. But that skier will stay in control if she feels confident. She will feel confident if she believes she is competent. She will believe she is competent if she has experience. It becomes a spiraling cycle, each step building toward the next continuously. Figure 12.1 illustrates this cycle.

There are ways you can build your confidence, even in things that are new for you or that intimidate you. You can build confidence, for example, in your ability to use the telephone to get more done to manage the calls you already handle. Confidence comes first from preparation. Be prepared by having what you need at hand, by knowing what you are going to say and do, and by having a goal for each call.

Competence comes with practice. You began practicing with your initial training and continued it with your first several months on the telephone.

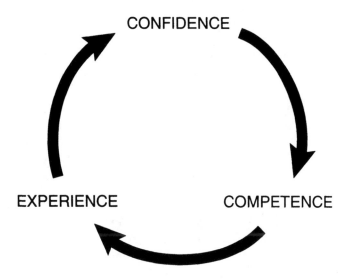

FIGURE 12.1. The Cycle to Self-Control

Now you are acquiring new communication skills. Translating confidence into a feeling of competence at managing the call and the other party comes over time. With a positive attitude and thorough preparation, you will improve on even your early calls. As you increasingly manage calls well, you come to recognize your own competence.

Competence enables you to handle more calls and more call situations. That translates into experience. Successful experience produces additional confidence. See where you are? The cycle begins anew. As you handle calls, you gain the experience needed to build your confidence. Increased confidence leads to a feeling of increased competence, which in turn leads to increased experience, and yet another increase in confidence. Your confidence ultimately lets you believe you can manage any call you make or receive. That belief makes for the self-fulfilling prophecy:

> You can manage any call you handle.
> Therefore
> You do manage any call you handle.

To overcome the mental barriers, then, you need to handle the calls. That is as true of your telephone work in general as it is of a single call.

Overcoming personal barriers requires you to realize that what you say and do reflects, first, on you. Every professional teleseller knows that effective, positive communication is more than the words spoken. It is a combination of the knowledge, enthusiasm, and appearance behind the words. It is a total attitude, conveyed to anyone with whom you are talking. The attitude is made up of several elements:

- *Concentration.*   Picture yourself handling each call with ease, skill, and success. Once into the call, focus on what you are going to do next. Concentrate on the present call, not on what you have done in past calls or what you might do in future ones.

- *Empathy.*   Assume, for the moment, the other person's point of view. Nowhere is this more important than in managing the various personal styles you encounter (see Chapter 11). Once you are able to envision the other person's point of view, you will find it easier to work with him to solve the problem your analysis of needs uncovered. This does not mean you always accept that point of view. But envisioning it will better enable you to work to persuade another person to your point of view.

- *Relaxation.*   When you sense you are not in control of a situation or anticipate losing control in the next call, you become tense and perhaps confused or distracted, losing your concentration. You are unable to perform at your best. To relax under pressure, take a deep breath or two. Flex a set of muscles for a few seconds, then relax them suddenly. Studies have repeatedly shown that the mind-body connection works both ways. Relaxed muscles do quiet the anxious mind.

You would also be well served to become aware of your habits, from self-observation or from comments from a friend or colleague. Break some of your old, ineffective habits. Learn of and try new ones. For example, examine your prejudices about prospects and customers or about your company's products and practices. Are you defensive about company procedures? Do you respond poorly to certain personal styles? Work to overcome those detected. To strengthen your performance, recognize your shortcomings. Plan for improvement by setting goals. Be patient as you work toward them, but start today. It takes sustained effort to minimize personal communication barriers that victimize you.

Overcoming verbal barriers also requires concentration. Take your time and do the job thoroughly each time. In this, your voice is obviously important. While you can't undergo surgery to change it, you can practice to improve it. At the same time, maintain an awareness of your word choice. Use easily understood, positive, action-inducing words. (*Note:* More tips on word choice and a teleselling voice appear in the two chapter sections that follow.)

And what can you do about physical barriers? Preparation is your key to controlling these. Have what you need at hand—no more and no less. In that way you won't lose control of your calls or interrupt the other party's thought process when you put the call on hold to go in search of a forgotten item or to look up information. But keep it simple. Avoid overburdening yourself to the point of erecting new barriers by having to shuffle through a mountain of materials and information as you talk.

Work to keep distractions to a minimum—not an easy task in a busy office, but worth the effort. When you sit down to a call session, be prepared to work the entire session without needless interruptions. This calls for both mental and physical preparation. You want to keep downtime to a minimum. That requires that you eliminate the physical obstacles you may have erected or that may have grown up around you. Your job during call sessions is to stay on the telephone as close to 100 percent of the time as is humanly possible.

In your effort to manage the course and outcome of each call, work at breaking the communication barriers with each person you contact. Use all the tools and skills at your disposal to keep you and the other person on track to a closed sale. You will seldom get a 100 percent meeting of the minds with each person, but when you practice the tips offered here, you will be able to capture the attention and interest of all types of prospects and customers. You are then in a better position to manage the entire sales interview to a successful conclusion.

Unfortunately, if you don't work to overcome barriers, there is no way to measure in precise numbers the impact that your poor communication techniques have on results. You can be sure that, to the extent you build or tolerate some of the barriers to communication discussed here, you are not managing your calls to the best of your ability. That costs you time, your company money, and your prospects and customers the satisfaction due them.

USING WORDS THAT SELL

Your ability to express an idea is as important as having the idea in the first place. Sales aids—pictures, fact sheets, samples, demonstrations, and the like—are traditionally used to express the idea of your product and what it does. Words are the only sales aids you have in teleselling.

Attention here will be on the types of words you can use to sell more effectively. And as you might expect, the best words are those that convey benefits. Benefits, you'll recall, show how a prospect is going to gain from acquiring your product. The words *benefit* and *gain* are themselves examples of effective selling words. Other examples of beneficial words include *guaranteed*, *ease*, *economical*, and *satisfactory*. What words, perhaps used in your product literature, can you add to this list?

_____

_____

Words that show your sincere interest in the needs, problems, and concerns of your prospect should also be included in your vocabulary. For instance, *appreciate*, *comfort*, and *useful* will tell prospects that you are thinking of them and not yourself. Again, pause here and add words that you will use in your dealings with your prospects to the list.

_____

_____

You have already read in this book of the need to be positive about yourself and your work (see also pages 176–180). Positive words inspire confidence in your prospect, too. Describe your company's service as *efficient*, your package as *complete*, and your company as *reliable*. Employ the principles of a Positive Mental Attitude in choosing how you describe your company and products, as well as in how you think about yourself and your work.

Telemarketing consultants Barry Z. Masser and William Leeds, in their *Power Selling by Telephone*, suggest you begin a "library" of words that invoke the image of action and, thus, get more sales. They assert that the words in the right-hand column of the following list invoke a far more positive response than do the words in the left-hand column.

effect	*impact*
versatile	*multifaceted, all encompassing*
interesting	*colorful, fascinating, riveting*
quiet	*soundless*
economical	*cost-effective*
up-to-date	*state-of-the-art*
complex	*elaborate, highly detailed*

emergency	*crisis*
capacity	*potential*
skill	*expertise, genius*
hopeful	*enthusiastic*
trim	*sleek*
surprise	*astonish*
good	*fantastic*
better	*superior*
energy	*force*
difficult	*formidable, tough*
produce	*generate*
popular	*renowned, distinguished*
inflexible	*rigid*
dismal	*ominous*
unusual	*exotic, radical*

This sampling should get you started at improving the action-invoking power of your selling vocabulary. Review what you plan to say. Use a thesaurus to find words you could substitute for some you planned to use, words that would make your speech more lively (make that *sparkling*). A word of caution: Don't look for bigger words, ones you could misuse. Just look for fresher or more vivid ones.

Always strive to be believable. Avoid superlatives. There can only be one *greatest, finest,* or *best,* and these are relative to needs and benefits anyway. Besides, all of these words are overused. Calling something the *newest* will only be accurate for a day or two in today's competitive market. Employing such a clichéd tactic can only erode the perception of accuracy you have been striving to establish. Believable words such as *dependable, excellent,* or *permanent,* when backed by some statement of proof, convey a positive image without you going to extremes.

Be sure to use words that reflect your enthusiastic attitude toward what you are selling. You are a *thorough* person, your product *complete,* and your service *exceptional.* Not only do such words convey your confidence and enthusiasm, they generate similar feelings in prospects. This will reassure them of the correctness of doing business with you.

Words that are descriptive of your product in use or that help the prospect envision the product are also important. Animated words, ones that dramatize the product and its benefits, will help you here.

In all instances, you want to select words that present your product in its most favorable light. A final tip to help you do this is to employ, where possible, the same terms used by the prospect in describing his or her needs. If, during the analysis, the prospect uses the term *trouble-free* to describe a desire for convenience, use that term when advocating your product. You may have planned to say *low-maintenance* or *maintenance-free*, taken from your sales literature; but in this case *trouble-free* will have a greater impact.

And to ensure that all benefits are evident to the prospect, use clarifying or summarizing phrases like, "What this does for you is . . ." or "For you, this means . . ." Again, wherever possible, use phrases, words, and expressions the prospect has mentioned as important.

Finally, choose precise words to get your exact meaning across. For example, instead of saying yours is a *good* company to do business with, you could describe it as a "reliable, capable, stable company with a history of service to its customers."

Does selling over the telephone mean that you can only describe your product and cannot demonstrate it? Numerous telesellers, to both consumers and businesses, do in fact put on demonstrations over the telephone. Some telesellers, like representatives for textbook publishers and stationery and greeting card manufacturers, send the actual product before the "ask for the order" call. Then they refer the prospect to the sample during the call. Others, such as photographic studios and housewares manufacturers, might precede the call with a sample and illustrative materials. And many companies send catalogs or similar collateral materials. What can you put in your prospect's hands, prior to your closing call, that will help you dramatize as fully as possible how your product meets his needs?

But placing an object (or literature describing it) in the prospect's hands does not relieve you of your obligation to present your products thoroughly and forcefully. And using such samples or materials means you have to be prepared to sell in two completely different circumstances: If the prospect has your literature or product in front of him, you will execute one call strategy. If your prospect alleges, correctly or incorrectly, that the material was never received, you must resort to a very different call strategy.

While on the subject of word choice, a consideration of jargon is appropriate. Every industry, trade, and profession has developed language and acronyms that an outsider cannot readily understand. While these terms and arrangements of letters have special meanings in your work and are used regularly when talking to co-workers, they are meaningless to others. For example, whether *Teleselling* is a "new-list" or "back-list" book that is "case bound" or "perfect bound" or "saddle stitched" means nothing to you as a consumer. But to its publisher such terms place it immediately within a range of products, and to its author they indicate likely readership and determine royalty rates. Using jargon such as this can and does confuse prospects.

Be sure to distinguish between jargon and legitimate industry phraseology, especially in business-to-business teleselling. The use of proper industry-accepted terminology enhances your professionalism and adds credibility to what you say. To avoid misunderstandings and the resulting dissatisfaction (or worse) on the part of the customer, you must use descriptive language that gets your exact meaning across. If technical language peculiar to your market helps to do that, use it. But be sure it is language your prospects will have no trouble understanding.

In addition to finding and using the correct words, you should be aware of your grammar and sentence construction. Either poor grammar or bad sentence structure will detract from your selling message just as much as inappropriate word choice, use of profanity, or any of the other obstacles described earlier. If you are unsure of yourself in either of these areas, a good handbook of basic English (available at any bookstore on or near a college campus) will give you the needed guidance. Keep one of these basic references at your fingertips for help with correspondence as well as with what you say.

Be conscious of the words you use and the message they convey. Reviewing the types of words presented here, plan your sales messages to pack the maximum punch. After all, your words carry the entire burden of expressing your sales message and getting you to your goal of closing sales.

A Teleselling Voice

Using the tape you were asked to make at the beginning of this chapter, listen to yourself and complete the two evaluation checklists shown in Tables 12.1 and 12.2 on page 152. (If you didn't make such a tape earlier, make it now.)

Realizing that yours is the voice of your company, how do you sound? Just as important, how can you go about acquiring the vocal characteristics you need? This, like other roads to self-improvement, starts with self-awareness and self-analysis. Listening to your own voice is the start. Now you must work to improve on what you heard in ways that will make you more effective.

A voice characterized by many of the positive qualities found on the two checklists just completed is a prerequisite for effective teleselling. The self-analysis you just completed was designed to help you determine your strengths as well as your weaknesses. Once identified, these will guide you in starting

TABLE 12.1. EXTEMPORANEOUS DELIVERY CHECKLIST

Indicate with a check mark those characteristics your speech exhibits or lacks during this activity:

Exhibits	Quality	Lacks
_____	enthusiasm	_____
_____	naturalness	_____
_____	interest	_____
_____	good pacing	_____
_____	knowledgeability	_____
_____	spontaneity	_____
_____	proper volume	_____

TABLE 12.2. VOICE-INVENTORY CHECKLIST

Regard each line below as a sliding scale from one extreme to the other. Indicate with a check mark where on each line you think your voice falls, judging by the test tape you made.

monotonous	_____	varied
harsh	_____	soothing
hostile	_____	friendly
contrived	_____	sincere
garbled	_____	clear
dull	_____	colorful
unpleasant	_____	pleasant
halting	_____	authoritative

your self-improvement program. Unless you have serious deficiencies in numerous areas, don't be put off. You don't have to be perfect, nor is it recommended that you retain an individual speech instructor (although a public-speaking course can help) or begin with oral surgery. Instead, work on the basics. Your goal is not to become a professional announcer, but to be a more effective teleseller.

One of the problems everyone faces to some degree when talking on the telephone is the tendency to talk in a monotone. This results from the fact that you are not face-to-face with the prospect and, thus, are missing the normal animation that occurs in conversation. Or it might be because you are delivering a scripted message or because you have repeated key points of your presentation so often that they've become just something you say. Frequent repetition of routine data during your analysis, answering often-raised objections, or filling out forms after you've gotten an order, can all sap enthusiasm from your voice.

To overcome a monotone, play a simple mental trick on yourself: Envision the prospect sitting across the desk from you. Talk to the image and not to the telephone. Also, vary your routine so you don't do everything the same way on each call you handle. Call different types of prospects—first leads, then cold calls, then customers—if you can. And remain enthusiastic. Each call is an opportunity for you to demonstrate your personal excellence, to solve a prospect's problem, and to close a sale.

Is your voice harsh, making you appear hostile or unfriendly? An antagonistic edge to your voice will put people off, resulting in a defensive attitude that will be hard for you to penetrate. Similarly, if your sincerity sounds contrived, either because it is or because you push your friendliness beyond acceptable bounds, you will raise barriers unnecessarily. A soothing, friendly, sincere voice will put prospects at ease, increasing their trust and confidence in you. To achieve that effect, begin by thinking a smile. If you then actually do smile while you are talking, your voice will assume a sincere, helpful tone that will encourage your listener to pay attention to what you say, as well as to build confidence in you.

Another potential problem for the untrained or undisciplined teleseller is rate of speech. How about you? Do you talk too fast or too slow? If you talk too fast, you are apt to give the impression that you are that stereotypical salesperson, the "fast talker." That will have devastating consequences for your credibility. And yet, slowing down too much is likely to make your prospect impatient, encouraging her to cut your call short.

You have two choices when determining how to pace your rate of speech: First, and preferred, is to match your rate to that of the prospect—speak in a slow and deliberate manner with those prospects who do likewise, and pick up the pace with faster talking prospects. If you haven't mastered that skill yet, aim for the middle: Vary your rate of delivery. Be crisp and businesslike when analyzing needs, methodical and patient when reviewing details, and enthusiastic when describing benefits or while asking for the order. In every instance, you want your rate of delivery to work for you, not against you.

Is your speech garbled? Do you talk too quietly to be heard or so loud as to annoy? All of these errors are common enough for you to be on guard against them. Do you chew gum while on the telephone? Or do you sneak a sip of coffee while the prospect is talking and then have to speak unexpectedly before you have swallowed it? These behaviors won't help your speech. Make sure your mouth is empty and speak in a distinct, well-modulated manner using a normal tone of voice. Speak directly into the mouthpiece and be conscious of your volume. Remember, the prospect is right across the desk from you.

Are you a colorful speaker? Do you create interest and draw attention when you speak? An expressive voice will help you get and keep the attention of your prospect. To be more expressive, raise and lower your voice, avoiding a monotone. Emphasize key words and phrases as needed. Vary your inflection and pitch to give variety to your conversation. Make your voice excited and vibrant so that it reflects your enthusiasm and helps build interest in what you are saying. The more enthusiasm and excitement you exhibit, the less canned you will sound.

The key to having a pleasant voice is to be natural. Don't try to force sudden or drastic changes, either on yourself or your voice. Learn instead to bring out the best in both. Being relaxed and natural is important if you are to project an image of sincerity. A forced speech or voice mannerisms will be apparent to the prospect and will damage your credibility. Instead, project a pleasant voice. Find your natural tone in the middle range of pitch possibilities. You can then manipulate the pitch up and down as the situation demands. Use the full range of the scale for maximum impact.

Finally, speak with the authority that comes from your positive attitude and self-confidence. You are, after all, the professional in the conversation. You know your product better than the prospect, and your prospect needs your product, perhaps without knowing it. You are the one trained in the skills of selling, and you are doing a job very few people can do well. Let those facts show in your teleselling calls. You are the expert.

In spite of the large number of calls you handle, you must sound fresh and credible, as though each prospect is the first and most important call on any given day. A well-developed voice will allow you to avoid giving the impression that you are mechanically running through a canned presentation. By delivering a natural sounding and enthusiastic presentation, from your "Hello" to your "Good-bye," you will close more sales. Once you can do this, you will appreciate the value of your voice as a tool.

The ideal teleseller will be able to project without shouting, will speak clearly and distinctly, and will deliver what is being said in a naturally pleasant manner.

ON YOUR OWN

1. Select one product you will be selling over the telephone. Gather all the relevant sales literature you can on that product. Organize the literature in a manner that you believe would be useful to you as you are talking about it on the telephone. Don't forget tabs, if they are appropriate, and highlighting with a marker to help you find just what you want when you want it.

2. Compile a library of action-invoking, believable, descriptive words and phrases you can use to describe that product and how it benefits a typical prospect (use the prospect you worked with in Chapters 6 through 9).

3. Create sentences you might actually use to describe the product and its benefits to the prospect. Rehearse them using either a tape recorder or the ear of a friend. Evaluate, or have your friend evaluate, your voice.

		Yes	No
SELF-INVENTORY	1. I have the materials I need on hand before I make calls.	____	____
	2. My vocabulary is appropriate to my task and my audience.	____	____
	3. I do not use slang, jargon, or unnecessary technical language in my sales interviews.	____	____
	4. I conduct my sales interviews in a spontaneous and enthusiastic manner.	____	____
	5. I maintain the highest ethical standards when representing my company and myself.	____	____

13 Effective Listening

THE KEY

Telephone communication, like all conversations, requires listening to what is said. Effective listening ensures that you learn everything you need to know in order to advocate an appropriate product. This chapter first demonstrates the effect your listening behavior has on others. Then you will learn whether or not you are listening to your prospects and customers. Finally, techniques are presented to improve your ability to listen. In this way you will uncover many more opportunities to make more, better, and larger sales.

WHAT EFFECT DOES LISTENING HAVE?

Many people, especially those who have never sold successfully for a living, have an image of salespeople as "good talkers" or, in the negative sense, as "fast talkers." They seem to believe that the term *con man* was derived from *conversation* rather than *confidence*. Sales professionals, though, know better. It is the effective *listener* who succeeds most often. And as a teleseller relying almost exclusively on oral communication, you must master this *receiving* skill to complement your *sending* skills if you are to maximize your success.

A simple exercise will demonstrate the substantial effect your listening behavior can have on your prospects and customers. First, identify by name a person whom you consider to be a good listener. Use a blank sheet of paper to record your answers to the following questions:

1. What behavior does this person exhibit that persuades you that he or she is a good listener?

2. What feelings do you experience when you are trying to communicate with the good listener you have in mind?

3. How do you behave toward the person you have identified as a good listener when you are trying to communicate with him or her?

Next, identify by name a person whom you consider to be a poor listener. On a separate sheet of paper, and substituting the phrase "poor listener" for "good listener," record your answers to the same three questions.

Compare your results. Did your list of the good listener's behaviors include such things as the ability to respond with appropriate questions or observations, the willingness to give you the time you need to talk, the ability to stick to the subject, the ability to be nonjudgmental, and the sense that you have his or her undivided attention? How about the person you described as a poor listener? Did your description of his or her behavior make mention of how he or she frequently interrupts you, asks a question that you've already answered, answers questions you didn't ask, won't let you get a word in, makes you repeat yourself, changes the subject, or tries to do two or three things at once?

And how do these two sets of opposing listening behaviors make you feel? Many people say that when trying to communicate with a good listener they feel important, comfortable, confident, relaxed, secure, trusted, as though they "belong" in the conversation. A poor listener, on the other hand, provokes frustration, anger, annoyance, a loss of interest in what is being said, rejection, boredom, and disappointment.

The most telling of three questions is the third one, about how you behave toward the good/poor listener. When in the presence of a good listener, people report they tend to be more polite, more open and forthcoming, a better listener themselves, calmer, and more willing to take the good listener into their confidence. With a poor listener, on the other hand, people report this behavior: They cut short what they are saying, hold back information, are impatient to be out of the conversation, utter irrelevancies to test the other person's attention, begin doing other things, pretend to pay attention, merely walk away, or, as more than one respondent has commented, "I avoid those people."

Look at the preceding paragraph again. If you exhibit poor listening behavior, look at the behavior you are provoking. Then ask yourself, "How could I possibly sell to someone who, having decided I am a poor listener, behaves toward me in this manner?" The simple truth is, if you do not listen, you will not sell.

ARE YOU LISTENING?

To become an effective listener, you must keep the difference between hearing and listening in mind. *Hearing* is a physical reaction to sound waves, wherein these waves are translated into understandable signals for the brain. You are hearing things at all times, some that you want to hear and many you don't. *Listening*, on the other hand, is an active process in which you consciously pay attention to what you are hearing.

In addition to the qualities of poor listeners identified earlier, the following behaviors are clues that indicate you are not as effective a listener as you should be:

1. You rely on heavy note taking, trying to get everything said written down. The goal becomes "get it down on paper," not "listen to what is being said."

2. You have little or no reaction to what the prospect is saying, but mechanically run through each call. The result: a lot of short calls.

3. You tend to tune the prospect out, race ahead mentally to what you will say later, or daydream about what you will do during your break.

4. You find yourself reacting only to preselected words or phrases that snap your attention back onto the call; then you wonder, "What did he just say?"

Your prospects will give you other clues that you are not listening:

1. Comments such as, "As I told you earlier . . ." or "I said . . ."

2. Frequent objections, which indicate you didn't hear the prospect's real needs and buying motives.

3. Fewer than average closed sales. You should, overall, close at least one qualified prospect in three.

4. Repeated questions from the prospect asking you to cover the same ground, indicating that you haven't heard what was really being asked.

If you detect any of these signals in your work, consider yourself properly warned that you aren't listening as carefully as you ought to be.

There are other behaviors on your part that become virtual *Interview Killers*. The following checklist was developed by *Specialty Salesman*, and repeated in Mona Ling's classic, *How to Increase Sales and Put Yourself Across by Telephone*. Are you guilty of any of the following behaviors?

	Yes	No
1. Finishing the prospect's sentence for her.	____	____
2. Inserting your own pet word or phrase if the prospect hesitates.	____	____
3. Trying to rush a prospect who speaks slowly.	____	____
4. Showing impatience at any time.	____	____
5. Educating your prospect over the telephone, which may invite questions you can't answer at that time.	____	____
6. Talking while the prospect is talking.	____	____
7. Failing to respond to indicators of attention or interest.	____	____
8. Estimating inaccurately the degree of emotional involvement or suggestibility in the prospect.	____	____
9. Projecting your own fears, opinions, insecurities, or thinking on the prospect.	____	____
10. Correcting the prospect midsentence.	____	____

If you put more than two checks in the "Yes" column on this activity or if you detected some recognizable signs in the poor-listening clues listed earlier, you'll want to give serious attention to improving your ability to listen.

TECHNIQUES TO IMPROVE YOUR LISTENING SKILLS

A lot of things interfere with your ability to listen effectively and to truly hear what is being said. The obstacles identified in this section are some of the more common ones with which you can easily deal without seeking outside help or making extensive changes in your work environment.

Avoid Interruptions

Inexperienced tellsellers seem to think it is necessary to talk to their prospects rather than listen to them. They may have been trained by someone who gave them bad advice, or they may be modeling their behavior after some of the poor salespeople they have encountered. Even when prospects assert themselves and try to say something, the teleseller may interrupt to express his own point of view. Then, when the sale is lost, the teleseller erroneously concludes that the prospect wasn't qualified. In fact, it was the prospect who was dealing with someone underqualified.

As you know from your own experience, interruptions are annoying and frustrating. You want to end a conversation that is frequently interrupted as soon as possible. In a similar way, if the prospect has something to say, you can safely conclude it is important to her. By cutting in or cutting off, you not only miss a key opportunity, you alienate.

A teleseller who has developed listening skills knows not to interrupt a prospect. If you are presently in the habit of interrupting, it will take self-discipline to overcome the tendency. Once aware of your tendency to interrupt, concentrate on not doing it. Strive to lessen the number of times you do so. Pause after each call, review how you behaved, and renew your vow not to interrupt the prospect unless it is absolutely necessary.

Concentrate

Another frequently encountered obstacle to effective listening is a lack of concentration, whether on your part or the prospect's. This can result from trying to do two things at once: Perhaps you are wrapping up the paperwork from a prior call while handling a new call, or you are having a snack while continuing to talk with prospects. What activities do you engage in while you are talking on the telephone? There is an endless variety of things you could be doing that break your concentration on the call you are handling at the moment. If you compile a list of things you do that interfere with your concentration, you will increase your awareness of this problem. It is important to control your work environment as much as possible to ensure it is free from distractions. Interruptions of all kinds should be kept to an absolute minimum. If you eliminate interruptions and distractions, you are free to concentrate on each call, one at a time, and on exactly what is being said.

Stay Fresh

Your attitude can also be an obstacle to effective listening. Do you get the feeling, "I've handled a thousand calls just like this"? Taking your work, prospects, or calls for granted, or behaving as though your activities will be routine, can lull you to sleep. Remember the phenomenon of the self-fulfilling prophecy: If you believe a call is going to be routine, it will be. With such a mind-set, you will stop listening.

Your best defense against this problem is to look upon each call as the unique teleselling opportunity it is. No two calls are alike. You know that. Be prepared to handle each call as a new, exciting, and separate activity.

Keep an Open Mind

Are you a prejudiced person? Do you hold a person's race, religion, sex, or national origin against him? Of course not. So why do you react as a bigot might when your prospect turns out to be a customer or prospect of your major competitor or when she is in an industry, activity, or area of the country where you have not been successful in the past? Product or market prejudice—jumping to conclusions about the likelihood of your success when you hear where your prospect is from or what his interests are, or who your competition is—can be a powerful barrier to listening. Instead of concentrating on what is being said, you tune out the prospect because you believe you are not going to get the order.

To overcome prejudice of any kind, you must keep an open mind. It is no different in selling. Take prospects as they come to you and realize you offer a valuable product for them to consider. If you are going to draw any early conclusions, let them be that the prospect will buy. But most important, listen for opportunities to sell. Overcoming objections and getting qualified prospects to buy is hard enough. Don't make it harder by deciding "no" for them before they do.

Be Enthusiastic

A final obstacle to listening could be your lack of interest in what you are doing or what you are selling. If your enthusiasm diminishes, if you are overly preoccupied with other things, or if you haven't made a sale in the last fifty calls, your interest in your work, your product, or your prospects can wane. When that happens, you stop hearing what is being said and begin reacting to your prior experiences rather than to what is really going on in the call you're on at the moment. A loss of interest can make it difficult to effectively hear what is being said.

If you find this happening, pause for a minute and take a deep breath. Take a brief break or go to another area away from your work station. Undertake a different activity—do some paperwork or move from selling to prospecting. Pull yourself together. You will only be as successful as your attitude and enthusiasm allow. Keep them intact.

Listening for Selling Opportunities

When you improve your listening skills, you will be able to hear more opportunities to sell. This can happen in several ways.

You will hear, for example, which benefits to stress and when to stress them. How many benefits could you apply if you were an automobile-insurance teleseller and heard a prospect say, "Well, but my current coverage expires in only three weeks"? Or if your cold call to an office manager, a prospect for your stationery company, produced the comment, "I always get my supplies from John Myer with Aaron Paper. He comes in on the first Monday of the month to take care of us"?

You will also hear many opportunities to create a need or desire. What would you say to create a need when you hear a prospect say, "I have enough of this stuff to last me the next six months. I'm overstocked already"?

Finally, you can learn, just from their conversation, what interests or concerns prospects most. Listening for what are referred to as "hot buttons," you will know which ones to "push" when advocating your product. What would you stress to a person who comments over and over again, "I am tired of doing business with companies that do not service what they sell"? (Service could be the real message when a person says, "Companies aren't run the way they used to be.")

List similar opportunities that your prospects present in what they say:

1. _____

2. _____

3. _____

4. _____

5. _____

How will you handle each of the opportunities you listed? Spotting the needs represented in prospects' comments and then presenting benefits to meet those needs is teleselling professionalism at its best. It demonstrates your interest in your prospects and their well-being, as well as your skill a providing service. Referring to the earlier selling opportunities, remember the following:

1. The person whose policy is about to expire will respond well to the benefits of your immediate coverage put into effect with a minimum of inconvenience. The monthly service feature of your competitor can be turned to your advantage if you ask how they get something they need between visits and point out that you are as near as the telephone.

2. Stress to the person with too much inventory that your automatic shipments, tied to order history and adjusted on the basis of each subsequent order, will ensure that they are never overstocked like that again. Ask if the money thus saved and the increased space made available for more inventory of a different nature couldn't translate into more and better sales for your customer.

3. Obviously, the repeated complaint offers you a chance to stress your toll-free number, twenty-four-hour answering service, or a similar provision of your company's marketing strategy, without having to ask the customer specifically about the importance of service. You have heard a need without prompting and then sold a benefit without even having to stress it.

One final plug, too, for the importance of a call strategy. Hearing and responding to these situations and to the ones you listed illustrates the need to have a call strategy committed to memory. Only when you automatically handle your strategy without conscious effort will your attention be free for listening for and hearing these all-important opportunities to sell benefits.

Listening is a two-way street. You can control your end of the communication bargain by concentrating on what you are doing; by keeping an open mind; by being mentally and physically prepared for each call; by demonstrating your interest in your work, product, and prospect; and by not interrupting. These qualities inspire the prospect to be a better listener as well. If you are enthusiastic and empathetic and make the effort to serve your customers' needs, you will find that your prospects pay attention to you. Your overall professionalism will then carry you to more closed sales.

ON YOUR OWN

This subject is so important that you are urged to do this exercise regularly.

1. Evaluate yourself using the Interview Killers (see p. 159) and the Self-Inventory included in this chapter.

2. Ask others to evaluate your listening behavior using the same Interview Killers.

3. After each of your calls, assess your listening behavior by summarizing the course and content of the call.

4. Ask yourself how the person you just called would answer questions 1 and 2 about you.

		Yes	No
SELF-INVENTORY	1. I review my listening behavior on a regular basis to ensure I am being a good listener.	____	____
	2. I keep my work area free from distractions, allowing me to concentrate on each call.	____	____
	3. I pay attention to what each prospect is saying throughout the call.	____	____
	4. I listen for unexpected opportunities to sell a benefit or create a need.	____	____
	5. I am conscious of both what is said and what is left unsaid, and I consider their total to be the prospect's message.	____	____

14 Managing Your Calls and Yourself

THE KEY

Perhaps the most difficult aspect of teleselling is not the telephone calls themselves, but the creation and maintenance of a level of organization, self-discipline, and positive thinking to sustain yourself in your work each day. All salespeople face rejection. In fact, their proposals are rejected more often than they are accepted. Telesellers are no different, facing rejection at about the same rate as face-to-face sellers. But the number of calls a teleseller handles each day—60, 80, or even 100 contacts in six to eight hours—means a much higher volume, if not rate, of rejection. To deal effectively with this phenomenon, skilled telesellers must be well organized and motivated to succeed, and they must think highly of themselves and of the work they do. This chapter provides you with strategies for organizing your workspace and sales tools. It then helps you set realistic productivity goals and stresses the need to control the length of your calls. Finally, it shares some basic techniques for building and maintaining a positive mental attitude.

ORGANIZING FOR SUCCESS

Your work area is your "home" while you are on the telephone. Have the following at hand, arranged in a manner that suits your work style:

- Your *telephone*, with a headset if one's available. The key pad should be accessible without your having to get up from your seat or stretch an inordinate distance.

- Your *computer and keyboard*. The screen should be easily and clearly visible, especially if you call up customer data, prompts as to how to respond to things the other person says, and the like. The keyboard should be as far from your telephone's mouthpiece as possible to minimize the distracting clack of you striking keys (silent keyboards are better, once you get use to there being no sound as you touch them).

- A *call binder or flip chart* that contains your scripted approach comments, features/advantages/benefits worksheets, and objections handbook (some of this may be computerized). If you employ entirely scripted presentations, those scripts, too, should be at hand for reference or review.

- A *clear space* immediately in front of you where you can lay out your file on the next prospect or account you want to contact.

- Optionally, *tools to help you see yourself* and/or the other person. One telemarketing organization, which sells exclusively to the elder market, has distributed a close-up picture displaying the faces of four older Americans. Many tellers keep a small mirror placed where they can see themselves shrug and smile before handling a call. A reminder of your Straight A's call strategy is provided for you to clip and post (see your Report Card on page 206).

- *Items to personalize* your space: snapshots of family or friends, plants or flowers, craft items and mementos, art your children made for you, pictures of things you want to buy with the incentive income you earn, whatever it takes to make you comfortable and aware of what or who—beyond yourself and your company—you are working for.

While we're on the subject of work area, and you are a part of your work area, let's establish a *dress code* (if your company doesn't already have one for you). If you are working from home, you're free to dress as you please. It is suggested, however, that you not sit in your pajamas or underwear while placing your calls. You are not "at work" in such attire, and you are almost certainly not dressed on par with the people with whom you are speaking. Such a deficiency cannot help but put you at a mental disadvantage. Dress for work using this guideline: Dress at least as well as the people you are contacting on the telephone.

Data Sheets

Accessible and readable prospect or customer information is critical to the success of your calls. A typical prospect or customer *data sheet* contains space for at least the following information:

1. Telephone number.

2. Fax number.

3. Name and address. If it is a company, it should include that of a head-quarters if the customer is a division of a larger organization and the parent company plays a role in buying decisions.

4. Key contacts, including room for their title and direct dial or extension telephone numbers.

5. Summary of the account's status (which of your products the customer uses and where it is presently purchased, for example).

6. Call history, containing brief notes on each contact made: when, with whom, about what, and so on.

Preprinted cards, pages, or complete folders containing space for such information can be purchased from a business supply retailer. Or your company may already have such forms. As you accumulate information about your prospect and customer, you should create a *file* for future reference and follow-up. Such files are best arranged alphabetically by customer name. Within each file, arrange the materials in chronological order, with the most recent activity or information on top.

Work Diary

A second filing system—a *work diary*—will be necessary for you to keep on top of the volume of work you handle by telephone. Such a system should include one divider for each month in the year as well as one divider for each day numbered from 1 to 30 or 31. Arrange the dividers so that the current month appears at front, followed by the numbered day dividers. At the back, in chronological order, arrange future-month files.

Using a daily "To Do" format—simple lined notebook paper with the month and day noted on top will do—create a sheet for each day as the need arises. When follow-up action is called for, pull the sheet for the day in question, note what you want to remind yourself to do, and then refile the sheet. If it is February and you must note to call Bronco Corporation on June 12, create a sheet for June 12, write the note to yourself, and file it in numeric order in the June divider. If your next call requires action later in February, go to that day's sheet (or create one) and note your intentions. Attach any needed documentation to the sheet before refiling it, making the daily dividers into a "pending" filing system.

At the beginning of a month, empty that month's file divider of its contents and distribute them among the day dividers. Then, at the start of a work day, you merely go to that day's divider and pull everything you'll need to begin work. (*Note*: Your work practices and/or company's policy may dictate whether you can leave an entire customer file in your daily divider. Certainly it is not recommended to create a dual filing system that results in you or others being unable to find critical information when it is needed. Give this careful thought, establish a practice, then stick to it without fail.)

Sales Kit

To enable the best use possible of your product knowledge, you should develop a *sales kit*. One of the advantages of telephone selling is that, as you give your talk, you are able to refer to written notes and printed matter, or to information on your computer screen, without distracting your prospect. Use the following suggestions as guidelines to help you develop such a kit. As you learn what works best for you, adapt your sales kit to the way you work.

1. *Keep it simple and easy to use.*   Unlike outside salespeople, you cannot afford pauses in the conversation. You have to be able to put your hands on the information you need quickly.

2. *Be well organized and consistent.*   Begin by dividing your sales kit into sections, preferably by product or product category. If you use a descriptive brochure, make sure you put one at the head of each section of your kit. Follow that with only such backup data as you will need—not everything anyone would ever want to know about your product, but what your experience and training tells you is likely to be important during the call. By using a uniform format throughout your sales kit, you will ensure that you are not distracted from your presentation because you can't find that missing piece of information.

3. *Use only marketing materials that work for you.*   You should feel free to tear apart the sales and marketing information you receive and to

reassemble it in a form that works for you. Discard what you find you have no need for, and put the remaining material together in a form that is easy to use.

4. *Let your experience on the telephone dictate your sales kit's content and format.* As you make your calls, be alert to the kinds of information you use repeatedly. How can you organize your sales kit to conform to the pattern of your calls? What questions do you hear asked? What objections do you encounter? What do your prospects say and when do they say it? How do they respond when you ask for the order? Keep the course and the content of your calls in mind while assembling a working sales kit.

5. *Keep it current.* Keep abreast of new developments in both your product and its market. As product improvements are introduced, additional uses identified, or new prospects uncovered, note them in your sales kit immediately.

The most important items in your sales kit are the features/advantages/benefits worksheets you develop. These worksheets will become the primary tool you use on the telephone. Therefore, be sure they are legible and in a location where you can put your hands on them immediately. At first, you may want to put a check beside a benefit block each time you use that benefit in a presentation. In that way, you can tell which benefits are most relevant for a product, and you can automatically integrate them into your presentation. Or you may want to work the most frequently used benefit into what you say to grab attention in your opening.

It is also important to note when you find yourself saying, "I'll find out for you and call you back." Each time you do, add the missing information to your sales kit. Looking up the answer, thinking about it in terms of its benefit to the prospect, and then writing it down will all help you remember what to say the next time.

Stop now and think about the items you must have at your fingertips in order to conduct a smooth, professional, successful sales call. In the following space, or on a separate sheet of paper, compile a thorough list of things you need to conduct the interview that your call context or call goal dictates.

1. _____

2. _____

3. _____

4. _____

5. _____

Did you include all appropriate company worksheets and ordering instructions? How about information sheets for the products you will be presenting? Are appropriate responses to objections or scripted responses (if used) readily available?

Preparing the Prospect

Attention should also be given to your prospects, who might also have to make preparations to take part in an uninterrupted interview. What things should they have on hand so that they can talk knowledgeably with you? What will they need so they can make a buying decision at the end of the interview? If you are selling automobile insurance, for example, your prospect will want to have her driver's license and vehicle registration for reference. If your prospect is purchasing computer supplies or software, he will need to know the make and model of his printers or the designation (Mac, DOS, Windows, etc.), version (6.07, 7.5, and the like), and capacity (2, 4, 8, 16, or more megabytes of RAM, etc.) of his operating system.

At the appropriate point in the interview, perhaps after prospects have said they'll buy, you'll want to ask them to get what is necessary to conclude the call. An individual consumer might need only a checkbook or credit card, whereas an organizational buyer might need a purchase order, authorization number, various shipping addresses, and more.

If such activity applies to your teleselling situation, compile a list of those items your prospects should have on hand to enable you to close the sale and call.

1. _____

2. _____

3. _____

4. _____

5. _____

The prospect might need little or nothing at hand in order for you to be able to conduct an effective call. But by taking the time to get both yourself and the prospect ready, you ensure fewer interruptions and greater concen tration on your sales message. To make it easier for you to set this up, stress to prospects that by taking a few minutes for them to get ready to discuss your product, you will take up less of their time and will be able to give them the best service and to recommend the most appropriate product.

Being well organized in everything from your desk top to your sales kit is not an end in itself. Rather, it is the means by which you achieve several goals, among them to be able to put your hands on what you need, when you need it, without fail, each and every time the need arises. Larger still is the goal of being as productive as possible using the minimum time possible. Perhaps the most important goal, however, is to demonstrate to your prospects and customers that you are a business professional who can be counted on to do the job right every time you are called upon to do so.

MANAGING YOUR CALLS

To effectively manage your calls, begin with a clear understanding of your call's objective. Call objectives are dependent on who you are calling, where your call fits into your or your company's overall sales and marketing strategy (a cold call, a follow-up to a mailing, a callback to someone who responded to your advertising, a solicitation for an appointment, and so on), what will happen after the call, and the purpose of the specific call. Depending on these factors, your call may last less than a minute or as long as twenty minutes.

These considerations supply answers to the three most frequently asked questions about teleselling procedures: (1) How many calls or sales contacts can one make in a day? (2) How long should the typical call last? (3) When is the best time to call?

The number of sales contacts you should expect to make in a day will depend on various factors:

- *The marketing context in which you are working and your call objectives.* If you are calling a list of suspects to qualify them as prospects, you will not need as much time per call as you would if you were conducting full presentations.

- *The quality of the list of names you are calling and how suitable they are to your call objectives.* Working from a telephone directory to sell to a homeowner or parent, you may complete a lot of calls but conduct few full presentations. But if you are calling a list of known customers to sell a pricing special, each call will take longer.

- *The product you are marketing and its complexity and the extent to which you must determine specific prospect needs in order to know which of a range of products to recommend.* If you are selling a set of books on a subscription basis, using a script and offering a free gift to buyers, you can complete more calls than if you are required to qualify prospects in order to determine which of your product models is best suited to their needs.

- *Other factors.* These can include the paperwork you have to do following each call and the amount of information you need to conduct the interview and its availability.

The following Call-Length Checklist and Call-Results Form (Table 14.1) should help you plan your work.

Call-Length Checklist

1. In what marketing context are you working?

    _____ cold-calling suspects

    _____ qualifying prospects

    _____ closing sales

    _____ providing customer service

    _____ other _____

2. What is your call objective?

    _____ to come up with a list of qualified prospects

    _____ to qualify prospects for appropriate sales literature

    _____ to make a full action-getting presentation to a decision maker

    _____ to ask for an order

    _____ to solve customer-service problems

    _____ other _____

3. How good is your list of names in relation to your objectives?

    _____ a broad, unqualified suspect list

    _____ a list of prospects to be qualified further

_____   a targeted list of qualified prospects

_____   a clean list of known users of the product

_____   other _____

4. How long should it take you to:

_____   quickly screen suspects to produce prospects?

_____   make a full presentation to qualified prospects?

_____   ask decision makers contacted for their order?

_____   other _____

5. How many minutes will each goal-successful call take?

_____   5 minutes

_____   10 minutes

_____   15 minutes

_____   20 minutes

_____   other _____

6. How many hours will you reasonably be able to put in per day on the telephone?

_____   3 hours

_____   5 hours

_____   7 hours

_____   other _____

Dividing the answer to question 5 above into your answer to question 6 (converted into minutes) will give you a preliminary answer to the question of how many calls to make in one day. However, go immediately to the Call-Results Form and begin to track your results. Your actual on-the-telephone experience will eventually provide you with the accurate answer to this question. Duplicate this form and begin filling it in each day you work. Over a period of time, even as little as a week, you will have an idea of what you can reasonably accomplish.

Of course, you should continually evaluate your work, looking for ways to increase your productivity. Can you change your attention-grabber, be

TABLE 14.1. CALL-RESULTS FORM

Teleselling activity	Mon	Tues	Wed	Thurs	Fri	Totals
Calls dialed						
Qualifying information obtained						
Targets contacted						
Active presentations made						
Order requests made						

more efficient in screening prospects, or take a worthwhile shortcut in your planned call course?

After a week of work, establish a goal for the number of calls you handle in a day. Then stay on the telephone until you reach or exceed the goal. After a month, as you become more adept at handling calls, you can increase your goal. In any event, don't fall short of your goal for any period of time (unless your experience shows it was unrealistic in the first place). Discipline yourself to complete the job, which means hitting your call goal every day you work on the telephone. Use success to motivate you to even greater productivity. Try to exceed your previous daily, weekly, or monthly high.

Closely related to the question of how many calls you can make in a day is the matter of how long the average call should last. This too will depend on your call objective. In a teleblitz—a large number of interviews made up of three or four key questions to identify qualified prospects from a list of suspects or general prospects—the calls are usually short. A teleseller at a travel agency may teleblitz suspects from a bought list of travel-magazine subscribers, asking how frequently trips are taken, when the next one is planned, where the trip is to, and (to prospects who meet preestablished guidelines, such as a trip planned within the next six months) if the person would like to be presented with several outstanding opportunities from the agency.

Close qualifying, followed by a full product presentation, answered objections, and a close, can take longer. The travel agent might call back to find out more about the just-qualified prospect's preferred activities, modes of travel, previous trips, choice of accommodations, types of experiences desired, and budget guidelines. Remember, though, no matter how extensive your presentation will be, you have only a few seconds in which to grab a prospect's attention. If you do that successfully, you can then take the time you need to achieve your call objectives.

Do keep in mind, though, that telephone calls are thought of as shorter encounters than talking face-to-face. You are expected to be brief. If you go beyond twenty minutes (and when possible, you should make your calls much shorter than that), you are not likely to be effective. The prospect's attention will wander or her irritation will rise. Keep it brief.

When is the best time to call prospects? Many tellesellers develop an elaborate rationale when trying to figure out the best time. In the morning, they will allow business prospects time to get their desks cleared and have their first cup of coffee. Then, of course, there is lunch. And if you call after 4 P.M., the prospect will be busy completing the day's workload. Consumers can't be called while getting children and spouses off to school and work, breakfast dishes cleaned, or dinner prepared. They can't be called in the evening for fear of interrupting dinner. Call between dinner and bedtime, but don't call on Tuesdays because . . . and so on and on. If you added up all these reasons not to call, you would conclude that there is less than one hour a day in which to make calls. And if the day you decide on is Wednesday, the week is practically shot. Oh well, maybe next week. . . .

Come on! The best time to begin calling is now! Other than not calling too early, say before 8:30 A.M., or too late, after 9:30 P.M., it is "store's open."

Most consumers cannot be called before 8:30 A.M. or after 9:30 P.M. without risking disturbing them and ruining your chances for a sale. If, when you do get through, you interrupt some important household activity, make an appointment or announce when you will call back: "I'm sorry to have interrupted your dinner. I'll get back to you in one hour, when you have a few minutes to talk."

Businesspeople often aren't in, or don't answer their telephones, before 9 A.M. or after 5 P.M. But even that isn't an absolute, and it may pay to try calling earlier or later. If you call someone and her work cannot be interrupted, you should make an appointment to call back at a more convenient time. If you repeatedly have trouble contacting a businessperson, remember that you are calling about something important to that prospect. Make an appointment to call back. Find out from the person screening calls when you could reach the prospect.

Get on the telephone at the start of your work day and keep at it until the day is over. Make the adjustments necessary for you to reach your contact goal, using appointments, call-return messages, or calling back yourself, as your experience dictates. Don't waste time finding excuses not to call.

If someone you contact expresses the desire not to be called again, respect those wishes. Take the steps necessary to remove the name from your or your firm's database, or at least flag it as one who does not want unsolicited teleselling calls.

Another phenomenon you'll need to prepare for is being answered by a machine. Do you want to leave a message? If so, will you leave specific information about the nature of your call? Or do you merely hang up? Remember that at least half of all people who own answering machines screen their calls, at least sometimes, with the machine. If you are going to leave a message, make it one of your best attention-grabbers: then ask for a callback. If, after a reasonable time has elapsed and no callback occurs, place your call again. Of course, track your results to learn which techniques work best for your products and markets.

MAINTAINING YOUR POSITIVE ATTITUDE

There are any number of reasons why you want to keep your spirits up about your work, not the least of which is that you want to get satisfaction out of what you do for a living and enjoy yourself doing it. Your results, in turn, will be reflected by your state of mind. With an improved state of mind about your work, your results will improve: greater work satisfaction and increased income. Not bad outcomes.

The first step in building a positive mental attitude is to acknowledge the need for it and then accept responsibility for your attitude and results at all times in your work. That plays to one of the attractions of work as a teleseller, the opportunity it presents to employ your entrepreneurial spirit. Regardless of the size of the organization for which you work, you are in business for yourself. You are a broker for products placed at your disposal by their maker and accompanied by the resources necessary to sell them. Facing the universe on your own, it falls to you to manage those resources and succeed or fail by your own devices. Your products are unique, and, because they are unique, there is reason to call every prospect imaginable to talk about them. Your belief in the company and the products represented and in the value of selling those products to qualified prospects makes it easier to get your selling message across. And don't lose sight of the fact that you are the most important factor in the sale. You are the difference between making and losing a sale.

To ensure that your careful planning will produce results, you now want to stick to that plan, confident in the knowledge that, if you do, you will be successful. As a professional writer commenting on his experience pointed out, "By merely setting goals, you have set in motion the force needed to see that they happen. When you set a goal and acknowledge it, you send the thought out into the universe. By so doing, you begin to make it come true." Using the answers you arrived at with the Call-Length Checklist and Call-Results Form, require of yourself that you reach the minimum number of prospects per hour. Set a success goal regarding the number of presentations you expect to deliver in that hour or the number of key decision makers you expect to reach. Keep at it until you do.

Use charts to track your results. Look at them every once in a while, and see that you really are getting the job done. Over an extended period of time—a month, a quarter, a year—you will see that you have contacted 2,400, 7,200, or even 28,800 prospects; made over 600, 1,800, or 7,200 presentations; and closed 200, 600, or 2,400 sales in those periods, respectively. When you get to feeling that a certain day just isn't working, look at your productivity charts and realize that if you just keep picking up the telephone, you will succeed. The large numbers of prospects the telephone allows you to contact guarantees that.

You should be aware of your attitude toward the telephone itself. If you were trained at or are active in outside selling, you may perceive the telephone as a threat to your livelihood. You don't need to. Nor, if you are new to selling and are using the telephone as your first sales channel, should you be intimidated by the instrument. It is only a tool for your work, like your paper, pen, or product kit. View it as outside salespeople view their automobile, a device that carries you into the presence of the prospect, thus doing little more than extending your legs electronically. And it does that more efficiently and effectively than any other medium available to you.

One of the first things that you have to sell a prospect on is yourself: You must persuade a prospect that talking with you is worth the time. One of your objectives, then, to be worked on throughout your teleselling career is to develop a personal public relations campaign. List the factors that you believe can help you sell yourself to your prospects:

1. _____

2. _____

3. _____

4. _____

5. _____

Remember that the company you represent and the products you sell will have an impact on your self-styled public relations campaign. And your campaign will be strongly influenced by the fact that you are selling by telephone and, thus, are not able to present yourself physically to the prospect. Your self-selling list should have included some or all of the following:

1. *Your image.* Earlier, you were presented with image as a factor in your calls. Image is created by things about you that lead a prospect to evaluate you even though you aren't visible.

2. *How you handle the calls.* Are you businesslike, behaving in a manner that reflects favorably on you and your company? If you hang up on annoying customers, argue with prospects, use profanity, or discuss controversial subjects, you are hurting your chances of making sales.

3. *Your coming across as a friendly, helpful person, confident about your ability to be of service.*

4. *Voice and speech mannerisms that make a favorable impression.* Remember the admonition, "First impressions count." What impression are you making?

5. *Making only positive statements.* You never make negative statements such as "I know you may not need this, but . . ." You also should never apologize for calling. You have a valuable product to offer. As an intelligent consumer, the prospect wants to be informed and, thus, allowed to make his own buying decision.

6. *Never calling the prospect by his first name.* This social error can be damaging. If you are having a drink with a prospect, calling him Bob would be okay. But as long as your sole contact is on the telephone, keep it businesslike and call him Mr. Jackson, unless invited to do otherwise.

7. *Being yourself.* You are part of the package that the prospect is buying. By being natural, you avoid appearing insincere and don't have to worry about maintaining some artificial role you assumed for the call.

These lists—yours and the one printed here—will serve you in keeping on track with a positive public relations campaign, selling yourself to the prospect at all times.

How do you deal with the long hours on the telephone, frequent rejection, and the sometime monotony of handling call after call after call? These problems plague all tellesellers, but are especially acute among those who work from a script. The following suggestions may help you:

1. *Take frequent breaks.* To facilitate keeping to your productivity schedule, tie breaks to your productivity goal, not the clock. After making sixty calls or thirty presentations, get up and go to another area, have a snack, get some exercise, or otherwise interrupt your routine.

2. *Vary your activity as it relates to your work.* Again reacting to your productivity and not the clock, follow a call-handling period with an administrative period, doing filing, note writing, or planning for the next session. If possible, do this in a work area away from the one in which you handle calls.

3. *Figure out ways to inject variety into the work itself.* Can you change scripts or parts of scripts? Can you work a different prospect or customer base or undertake a different marketing activity, shifting from cold-call prospecting to customer service? Any change of work pace will help get through the three or four hours you put in on the telephone at any one time.

This is perhaps the appropriate place to consider one aspect of teleselling that concerns many who are new to the work. You have no doubt heard there are people—you, perhaps, were one of them before starting this work—who have a hostile attitude toward tellesellers. When you encounter such people, there are several things to keep in mind.

1. You can be confident that almost every adult in America has bought something by telephone. This is not meant to contradict the Direct Marketing Association's statistic that "55.2 percent of America's adult population ordered merchandise by mail or phone in 1993." Here's why: That statistic does not include many of the everyday things people order by telephone, such as the home delivery of pizza, the making of a reservation at a restaurant, or the telephone "ordering" of money from an automated teller machine (ATM). If these and similar activities were included in the purchases made by telephone, as they should be, virtually everyone in the nation would have to acknowledge their favorable predisposition to buying by telephone.

2. To those who say, "Yes, but you tellesellers always call at a bad time," there are two responses. First, many good ideas for satisfying needs come

at inopportune times. And, unlike a string of commercials in the middle of a favorite television show, telesellers are more kindly disposed to being asked to call back at a better time. Second, and more important, the prospect who says this is not saying she is not interested. In fact, what she is saying is, "I'd like to know more, but can't talk now." That is the perfect opportunity to make an appointment for a callback later.

3. People who are hostile to telesellers are probably hostile to salespeople of all types. They throw away their direct mail, or send back a blank response card, as if running up the costs of doing business benefits anyone. They grumble about retail salespeople at every opportunity, at least until they need a question answered. And they hang up on telesellers, sometimes preceding that event with profanity. Pity them. You know more about your product and how it can be used to the prospect's maximum benefit than anyone the prospective customer is likely to encounter. Most people will, if your precall homework adequately determines that your calls are going to qualified prospects, welcome the opportunity to talk with you and learn about how what you have can help them.

Finally, enable yourself to continue to grow professionally and personally by maintaining a reading program. Reading books and magazines by and about successful telephone or face-to-face salespeople, such as those listed in Sources for More Information (pages 207–209), will boost your confidence in your own abilities. It will provide reinforcement when you learn that other pros do the same things you do. More important, it will provide plenty of tips on what works. Whether you relate to, say, items 3 and 7 from a list of ten successful closes or to an entire strategy for penetrating a new market, you can plug what you read in to what you encounter on the telephone. Feeding ideas to your brain in this manner will help you when you encounter new situations, different people, and related activities.

ON YOUR OWN

1. Select a customer file at random, or create a new one by labeling a manila folder with a prospect name.

2. For an established customer file, go through the items it contains. Select the items that are critical to a full understanding of the customer and a history of his relationship with your company. Discard extraneous materials. If necessary, rearrange the materials into chronological order as suggested in the opening section of this chapter.

3. For a prospect file, make a list of all items you will need to give you a complete picture of the prospect and enable you to plan your first contact. Where can you acquire what you've identified as critical? Assemble the needed materials.

		Yes	No
SELF-INVENTORY	1. I keep all relevant sales literature readily at hand for me to consult as needed while I am on the telephone with the prospect.	___	___
	2. I have my call objective clearly in my mind before I pick up the telephone.	___	___
	3. I discipline myself to put in the time, energy, and work needed to be successful.	___	___
	4. I put myself in a positive frame of mind about myself, my company, and its products before I make each call.	___	___
	5. I handle each call in a way that represents my best effort and highest professionalism.	___	___

15 Developing a Script

THE KEY

You have been urged throughout this book to employ a flexible, planned, but extemporaneous sales-call strategy whenever you can. There are, however, situations where a script might suit your needs or goals. This chapter presents you with the relative merits of scripted calls versus extemporaneous sales calls, provides you with guidelines for preparing scripts, and demonstrates scripting in action with two representative samples.

THE PROS AND CONS OF SCRIPTED CALLS

A flexible, responsive approach to the content of your sales call is a virtual requirement when you are teleselling to the business community and, thus, are calling on knowledgeable or professional buyers. Teleselling a sophisticated product to individual consumers also can require that you adapt your presentation to suit various prospects and situations. However, such activities as lead generation, trial offers, post-sale follow-up, and replenishing or replacing supplies or parts, and such goals as qualifying leads, securing appointments, and making one-call closes can be handled quickly and easily by both veterans and new tellers using a script.

A long-running debate in teleselling concerns the importance and value of scripted selling messages over planned but extemporaneous presentations (as described in Chapter 7). The cause of this debate is that scripting offers a number of unique, even enviable advantages over the extemporaneous approach to teleselling.

People who favor a script for the entire presentation point out the following *advantages*:

1. *Anyone can deliver a script.*   With a minimum of training and start-up time, additional tellers can be hired, or a service company can be used with scripts that have been tested and proven.

2. *There is better control over the quality of the call.*   If you are working with other tellers, you can be sure each of you is delivering the same presentation, making the same offer, and asking for the order—all in a way proven by testing to be successful.

3. *You won't forget something important.*   In handling a large volume of calls and interacting with many different prospects, possibly under pressure, it is normal that key features are sometimes slighted or skipped during the presentation. Scripting avoids this possibility.

4. *A script ensures effective time management.*   If you expect to complete a set number of calls per hour, the script removes the temptation to digress, initiate small talk, or otherwise drift into conversations that take longer than planned.

5. *You can measure the variables in your presentation more easily.*   By making changes in the script that affect how such things as key benefits, the price offer, or incentives for acting now are presented and by keeping accurate records of the results, you can determine almost immediately what works best—if benefit A induces more favorable responses than benefit B, or if stressing a discount gets better results than a low base price.

6. *You exercise maximum control over the course of the call.*   You initiate questions where *you* want or need them, head off objections, and phrase benefits for maximum effect, allowing you to better direct the call to your desired result.

7. *A script can increase your confidence in yourself.*   A script can put your mind at ease if you are uncertain of your skills. This is especially important for someone new to teleselling.

8. *A script allows you to quickly achieve a very limited goal at minimum expense.*   For example, when conducting a teleblitz to learn whether or not a suspect meets the criteria necessary to become a qualified prospect, a brief, scripted call covering all the teleseller's concerns would be the cost-effective way to go.

But scripted delivery has its *disadvantages*, too. You should consider them before you make up your presentation. They include:

1. *A scripted message can come out sounding like the canned pitch it is—*especially after numerous deliveries, when it becomes second nature.

2. *The prospect you are calling might not really fit your script,* which might miss the mark completely and address benefits that are not important to that individual. This will be immediately obvious to the prospect, and the teleseller will get tuned out.

3. *Today's sophisticated buyer might see the script as an attempt to fit the prospect to the teleseller's preconceptions* rather than to fit the product to the prospect's needs.

4. *The teleseller's credibility as a problem solver, interested in the prospect's needs and concerns, might be undermined.*

5. *If the script misses the mark and unanticipated questions arise, you might be in a jam.* A script inhibits creative, free-thinking responsiveness on the part of the teleseller.

6. *A canned pitch might be viewed by many prospects as condescending.* And you might appear artificial and insincere, as if you have a low opinion of the intelligence and creativity of the prospect.

7. *The script might pack too much into the presentation:* too many benefits, an overwhelming array of data, even answers to common objections that the prospect wouldn't have thought of if you hadn't brought them up.

8. *A script that is inflexible can lead you to be that way, too.* Say to a teleseller using a script that you want to buy his product in the middle of his scripted message, and listen to the shuffling pages as he struggles to find out what he is to say next.

The decision whether to script your presentation should be made only after weighing the pros and cons mentioned and applying each to your own marketing and call strategies.

Earlier you were urged to make a script of your attention-grabbing approach. That is important in order to get all of the elements of an introduction, including at least one attention-grabbing Initial Benefit Statement, before your prospect in just twenty seconds. A script that is carefully planned, rehearsed, and delivered word for word is crucial to your opening.

DEVELOPING EFFECTIVE SCRIPTS

A scripted presentation must meet several criteria if it is to be successful: (1) The style must be conversational, that is, organized and worded in such a way as to appear to be a natural dialogue between teleseller and prospect. (2) It must be interactive. You are not making a speech. Provision must be made for prospects to participate—ask them questions, allow them to respond positively or negatively to certain options or possible courses of action, ask for their reaction, and so forth. (3) The fact that you script your call does not alter the need to follow a stepped-call strategy—the Straight A's—which leads from grabbing attention through a demonstration of your understanding of prospect needs, advocating a product, and asking for the order. As you create your script, refer to the principles presented in Chapters 5 through 10.

A well-written script begins with a clearly stated call objective. Use this space to write out, in one sentence, the objective of the call you intend to script:

_____

_____

Once you have established your call objective, use the following outline to create your scripted message. It follows the Straight A's call strategy step by step. It identifies the goal of each step. It summarizes what is to be accomplished in each step. And it allows you space to create your scripted copy. Use additional sheets of paper as necessary.

Step 1:   **Approach**

Goal: To secure the attention and interest of the prospect and the time to present your product for consideration.

Cover: a. Introduction: your name and your company's name.

　　　　　　b. Initial Benefit Statement: the reason for your call, including mention of your product by name, how it will benefit the prospect, and proof of the benefit.

Copy: _____

　　　　　　_____

　　　　　　_____

_____

_____

Step 2: **Analyze Needs**

Goal: To learn the prospect's problems and concerns and to create needs and desires, all to help you select and advocate an appropriate product.

Cover: a. Ask closed questions to gather data.

   b. Ask open questions for amplification and clarification.

Copy: _____

_____

_____

_____

_____

Step 3: **Advocate a Product**

Goal: To present product(s) you recommend in terms that satisfy prospect needs and buying motivations.

Cover: a. Renewal of interest: Select a suitable presentation opener.

   b. Transition and body: Make your product recommendation, stressing benefits you know will satisfy needs and desires.

   c. Close the point: Summarize and employ a trial close.

Copy: _____

_____

_____

_____

_____

Step 4:   **Answer Questions and Objections**

Goal: To remove the obstacles to getting the sales action you want.

Cover: a.   Restating the objection: To be sure you understand it.

b.   Qualifying the objection: Ask questions to analyze the causes of the objection.

c.   Answering the objection: Stress benefits.

d.   Close: Secure agreement with your response.

Copy: _____

_____

_____

_____

_____

_____

Step 5:   **Ask for the Order**

Goal: To achieve your call objective as a natural conclusion of the call.

Cover: a.   Closing techniques: Use an appropriate technique to secure agreement.

b.   Go back: Employ a strategy to address any objections that surface this late.

Copy: _____

_____

_____

_____

_____

_____

Step 6:   **Apply Service**

Goal: To take the steps necessary to insure prompt and proper fulfillment and to set up future contact.

Cover: a. What has been agreed to: Summarize the order.

         b. What will happen next: Outline completion of the terms of the sale.

         c. Show appreciation: Say, "Thank you for your order."

Copy: _____

        _____

        _____

        _____

        _____

        _____

Once you have completed filling out your outline, you can use your copy in one of two ways. You can assemble it, word for word and in strict chronological order, as text (see the examples in the next section). Or you can excerpt appropriate phrases and/or sentences and arrange them as bulleted lists for your reference throughout the call. Again, your experience as a teleseller as well as the purpose and context of the call will dictate which approach is best for you at this time.

A script is, by necessity, a dynamic mechanism. The emphasis you give each aspect will depend on how well you know the prospect, whether or how well the prospect or customer knows you and/or your company, and the context and objective of your call. And through repeated rehearsals, rewrites, tests on a sample of its intended audience, and more rewrites, you want to get it perfect before rolling it out to your overall market.

Even then, you must give consideration to the fact that, in business to-day, change is constant. New products from your company, new competitors, new products from competitors, news uses for products from you and your competitors, not to mention the multifaceted changes occurring in your markets, all make it necessary to review what you have scripted on a regular (if not daily) basis. When a change that impacts your sales and marketing effort occurs, corresponding changes to your script must be made.

TWO SCRIPTS

A consulting firm developed the following script for use by telesellers in securing appointments for its outside salespeople. The telesellers might use such a script verbatim; or they might use it solely for training, conveying the message in their own words once they are on the telephone.

(TO OPEN) Hello, Mr. Wallace. I'm Steve Johnson with MMS, Incorporated. We specialize in management development systems tailored to the food-processing industry. Such clients as Kellogg's, French's, and Hanover Brands have documented increases in productivity as high as forty percent when using our techniques. I'm calling to share those techniques with you.

(REGARDLESS OF PROSPECT'S RESPONSE) Well, fine. To better determine which of our materials can serve you, I'll need answers to a few brief questions. How many employees does your plant have? (PAUSE) How many supervisors do you employ? (PAUSE) Then each supervisor manages the work of _____ employees. Is that right, Mr. Wallace? (PAUSE) Do you presently make use of the employee participation concept, such as Quality Teams, in company decision making, Mr. Wallace? (PAUSE)

(IF "YES") How has that worked for you? (IF NO DISSATISFACTION WITH PRESENT PROGRAM, DISENGAGE AND HANG UP.)

(IF "NO") Have you ever considered using such a program?

(IF "YES") Which one? (PAUSE) That is an excellent program. Given its wide acceptance and good results, why was it not implemented?

(IF "NO") Mr. Wallace, the MMS Team Builder program has shown, in numerous companies in your industry, that it can reduce absenteeism and turnover, increase productivity, moderate labor tension, and improve morale. Which of these problems are your greatest concern? (PAUSE) Are there any other factors at work in your company that you feel are also limiting your workers' ability to produce to their maximum potential? (PAUSE) Would you elaborate on why? (PAUSE)

Mr. Wallace, you are right to include management attitude as one of the barriers to implementing an employee participation program and improving your plant's productivity. MMS Team Building starts with management. Our service includes two full days of orientation to insure that top management at your firm has a positive attitude and realistic expectations of the program. And we follow up with intermittent reports to top management on the progress we are making with your people. Would you agree that this initial step and our follow-up will solve the management attitude problem for you? (PAUSE)

(IF "YES," CONTINUE.)

(IF "NO," ASK "WHY" AND ADDRESS.)

Another benefit of the MMS Team Builder concept, growing out of our unique "Team Form" procedure, deals with your concern about an immediate positive impact on morale. This in turn reduces absenteeism, labor/management tension, and, in the long run, turnover. Are those your most pressing concerns? (PAUSE) Trained MMS personnel conduct initial sessions with all affected employees to solicit participation. These same MMS staff members then train your team builders and conduct the first team meeting. You benefit in three ways:

First, you can begin reaping the benefits of employee participation on day one, while preparing to eventually take over the full program at your own pace.

Second, your people are trained on the job, not in a classroom. They gain invaluable hands-on experience. They learn to deal with their own work and problems, not hypothetical situations. And the workability of the program is demonstrated to those who are key to its success, the workers themselves.

Third, you save money. All our development programs take place on site. You do not have the expense of sending people to seminars in faraway cities, and you do not lose valued employees at perhaps critical times.

Aren't those among the benefits you sought when you looked at other employee participation programs, Mr. Wallace? (PAUSE)

(IF "NO") What else were you looking for? (PAUSE) (CLOSE AND GO ON.)

(IF "YES") Mr. Wallace, I will have a representative in Cincinnati next week. I would like her to sit down with you and share our employee participation techniques and program with you. What day would be most convenient for you? (PAUSE)

(IF DAY IS GIVEN, SECURE APPOINTMENT AND DISENGAGE.)

(IF "WHY DON'T YOU SEND ME SOME LITERATURE ON 'TEAM BUILDERS?' I'LL LOOK IT OVER AND GET BACK TO YOU.") The brochures covering all aspects of this program total twenty-seven. Mr. Wallace, I know you're a busy man. Do you have time to read through twenty-seven detailed brochures by next week? (PAUSE) And one key benefit of the MMS Team Builder is its adaptability to each client situation. When you have installed the program, it will be unlike any of the more than 120 others we have in place. Wouldn't you find it easier to spend twenty minutes with our representative? (PAUSE)

(IF "YES," SET APPOINTMENT.)

Thank you for your time Mr. Wallace. Ms. Kelly will see you next week at _____. If others in your company should attend, invite as many as ten people, those you think may be involved in the decision. We look forward to your reaction to our unique concept. (DISENGAGE)

The following script was developed by a firm that publishes financial planning materials for individuals described as "well to do." It is intended to secure orders for a new publication and employs the "offer close."

(TO OPEN) Hello, Mrs. Curtis, I'm Fran Bailey with Hester and Ernst, financial publishers. I'm calling you because your subscription to our *Financial Planning Report* leads me to believe you would benefit from our new *Financial Independence Manual*. Are you mapping a financial strategy to make yourself financially independent within ten years, Mrs. Curtis? (PAUSE)

(REGARDLESS OF THE RESPONSE) Well, fine. Our new *Financial Independence Manual* shows you how to plan for and control every type of personal financial need. Developed by our expert staff, under the supervision of noted financial planner Calvin Roberts, it includes nearly three-hundred user-tested forms, reports, sample spread sheets, charts, and analyses for your use. Our *Financial Independence Manual* helps you plan and monitor cash flow, asset growth, and investment returns. Do you do your financial planning on paper or on a personal computer? (PAUSE)

(REGARDLESS OF THE RESPONSE) The reason I am calling now, Mrs. Curtis, is that the *Financial Independence Manual* is ready for your examination on a thirty-day approval basis. I'd like to send you a copy to look over on that basis. Over the next thirty days, you can use it and see that it suits your needs. Would you prefer that I ship a hard copy or a CD-ROM?

(IF "YES," CONFIRM COMPUTER REQUIREMENTS AND ADDRESS AND DISENGAGE.)

(IF "NO") Mrs. Curtis, you'll be pleased to know that the Manual comes in its own box, suitable for return shipment. And we include a postage-paid, preaddressed label to cover return postage. Should you decide the Manual is not everything you expect or want, there is no cost or obligation, or inconvenience, to you. Won't you avail yourself of this opportunity and okay delivery? You can then see for yourself how useful the *Financial Independence Manual* can be to your effort to reach financial independence. (PAUSE)

(IF "YES," CONFIRM ADDRESS AND DISENGAGE.)

(IF "NO," DISENGAGE.)

The scripting of telephone sales messages has its place in telemarketing. The key, though, is to use scripting selectively to address specific needs and situations. Once you have determined that a scripted message is the most effective way to handle a specific situation, develop and use one. But don't approach your teleselling work determined to use scripts in each and every circumstance that arises.

ON YOUR OWN

1. Select a product and identify a group of prospects for that product.

2. Establish a call objective for your initial contact with those prospects about your product.

3. Create a script, covering the Straight A's in teleselling, that you believe will accomplish your objective with that prospect group.

4. If possible, get on the telephone and test your script for its effectiveness.

		Yes	No
SELF-INVENTORY	1. The scripted format is appropriate to my purpose.	____	____
	2. My script includes opportunities for the prospect to talk at regular intervals.	____	____
	3. I take steps to ensure I am not talking in a monotone when delivering my scripted message.	____	____
	4. My script successfully incorporates the steps in the Straight A's call strategy.	____	____
	5. My objective for the scripted call is specific and clearly stated.	____	____

Performance Evaluation Survey

The traits and abilities in the following table are of prime importance among those you will need to succeed as a teleseller. Rank each factor, using the number that best reflects your assessment of your own work. After you have filled in all the blanks, add each column and record the totals for future comparisons.

Importance		Level of Performance
None	5	Rarely
Little	4	Occasionally
Average	3	Average
Significant	2	Frequently
Vital	1	Every time

Factor	Importance	Level of Performance
1. **Mental Comfort:** I am in a positive frame of mind. I believe I have a valuable product to offer.	____	____
2. **Physical Comfort:** I have at hand all materials needed to make a sale. I ask my prospects to get what they'll need at hand before I begin.	____	____

3. **Precall Planning:** I know what I'll say in each situation I'm likely to encounter. I know what information I'll need and where I can get it. _____ _____

4. **Nervousness:** I do not reveal any nervousness when talking to a prospect. My speech is clear and word choice appropriate. My voice is under control. _____ _____

5. **Voice:** I don't talk in a monotone. I don't talk too fast or too slow. Prospects hear and understand me. _____ _____

6. **Selling Strategy:** I always follow a system of basic selling steps. I prepare and deliver an orderly, easy-to-follow sales call. _____ _____

7. **Enthusiasm:** I take a strong interest in my products. I work for a good company whose products are important to people. _____ _____

8. **Attention-grabbers:** I use a strong opening remark to get the prospect's attention. I avoid jumping to conclusions that block my effectiveness. _____ _____

9. **Sales Message:** I am mentally prepared to respond to any situation when I pick up the telephone. In my selling, I stress what my product will do for the prospect. _____ _____

10. **Listening:** I concentrate on the call I am handling and avoid distractions. I don't interrupt my prospects. _____ _____

11. **Adaptable:** I react to the type of person I am calling, tailoring my manner and message to the prospect's. _____ _____

12. **Analysis:** I know what questions to ask to create listener interest. I learn the prospect's needs and wants. I get the whole story. _____ _____

13. **Word Use:** I have good enunciation and an extensive vocabulary. I use selling words. I evoke clear mental images and avoid using jargon. _____ _____

14. **Advocating:** I sell the benefits of my product. I am enthusiastic. I stimulate a need or desire to buy. _____ _____

15. **Flexibility:** I can put together quickly an action-getting sales message that is tailored to a prospect's personality and needs. _____ _____

16. **Answering Objections:** I react positively to objections, addressing and disposing of one objection at a time. I employ a "price is value" strategy. _____ _____

17. **Asking for the Order:** I get the sales action I set out for. I am alert for buying signals and employ the trial close and other closing techniques. _____ _____

18. **Control of the Interview:** I try to control the course and content of each call. I stick to my plan and urge my prospects to do so when necessary. _____ _____

19. **Paperwork:** My work is planned.
    I am well organized. I keep my
    commitments and complete all
    necessary paperwork on time and
    according to instructions.   _____   _____

20. **Sales Goals:** I have daily goals
    and other periodic goal checkpoints.
    I regularly reach or exceed my quota.   _____   _____

21. **Applying Service:** My attitude
    is to serve my customers and
    prospects in all of my dealing
    with them.   _____   _____

22. **Product Knowledge:** I can
    distinguish among features,
    advantages, and benefits. I
    understand buying motives and
    the importance of selling benefits
    to meet those motives.   _____   _____

Now that you have completed the Performance Evaluation Survey, you have a measure of your attitude toward and proficiency in the skills needed to succeed at teleselling. Clearly, each factor listed is important in teleselling. How important it is to you will depend on the selling activity in which you are engaged and the product you are selling by telephone (for example, applying service [Item 21] will be less important in a one-call-to-close situation than it will be in multicall, relationship-building selling). In general, however, the higher "Importance" you attach to a skill or attitude (and, thus, the lower the number you assign it), the more desirable it is that your "Level of Performance" score equal or better the number you place in the "Importance" column.

You should, from time to time (perhaps every three or six months), complete the questionnaire again. By comparing your score with the last one, you can evaluate your progress in strengthening your work on the telephone. Completing the test on a regular basis can also serve as a quick check to ensure that you are continuing to develop your skills in the right direction.

Afterword

Completing this book has gotten you off to a solid start in your teleselling career. If you already sell but are now moving into teleselling, this book no doubt brushed up your selling skills and made you aware of the differences between face-to-face and telephone selling. But remember, this is just the beginning. You have come far enough now to see other selling-skills books (especially those that urge numerous steps, keys, or secrets) in their proper light: as guides for possible behavior in situations that might (or might not) apply to your selling. Read those books and any other magazines, newsletters, and publications that can help you in your work. Attend seminars. Study salespeople you know and admire. Talk with your peers.

Telephone selling is an exciting field, one that is going to continue to grow and change in the future. It will be up to you to stay in command of effective new techniques and on top of your profession.

A Sample Mail-and-Phone Program

A manufacturer of luxury automobiles, in recognition of the fact that its primary market—doctors, lawyers, and corporate executives—were either unable or unwilling to come to its showrooms to shop for a car, introduced a "house calls" program for its dealerships. The essence of this program is that qualified prospective buyers, by making an appointment, can arrange to have a sales representative bring a showroom model of the car to their place of employment (or home) for a full, personal presentation of the car's features and to experience a test drive. The elements of the program include:

1. Broadcast and print advertising for use in local media. It shows, for example, a helicopter flying along with the car suspended by a cable underneath. This dramatizes the fact that the automobile company is willing to bring the car to the buyer.

2. Expensive brochures with discrete matching envelopes and stationery.

3. Compiled lists with the names, addresses, and telephone numbers of the target market printed on both mailing labels (although it is recommended that the envelopes be individually addressed) and file cards.

Ultimately, the effectiveness of this campaign—its success or failure—rests with the individual sales person. To facilitate the sales representatives using these materials (which are paid for by the dealership), a further mail-

and-telephone campaign has been introduced. It consists of the following steps:

1. Mailing labels are divided equally among the sales representatives of the individual dealerships and generally cover all prospects within a 100-mile radius of the dealership.

2. The text for a half dozen sales letters (see representative sample on page 201) is provided on disk for use on word processing equipment at the dealership. The sales representative is to select one or more of these letters for use in the campaign. The dealership then prints the letters over the sales representative's signature and addresses the envelopes.

3. The sales representative then supervises the mailing of these materials as a prelude to a telephone call soliciting an appointment to demonstrate the automobile. The salespeople are instructed to mail in a week only the number of letters (usually twenty-five) they can conveniently follow up with a telephone call four business days later (*Note:* The number twenty-five is based on the anticipated volume of calls that a salesperson could handle in one morning, while doing other work, and on the likelihood of having to make eight to ten demonstrations a week as follow-up to the letters and telephone calls.)

4. The sales representatives maintain and use careful call records (see Table A.1 on page 202). These call-record forms allow the salesperson to track this specific sales activity individually; make possible an easy-to-maintain-and-follow call-diary system for tracking prospective buyers presently in the market for such a car, as well as those who might be in the market in the future (and when that would be); and enable management to determine the overall effectiveness of the house calls program.

The house calls program demonstrates how the telephone can be used effectively to take over part, if not all, of the selling process; the part in this case is cold-call prospecting. Outcomes of the house calls program have been dramatic. Many dealerships report that sales of new cars increased so much that many dealership owners have introduced similar programs for other models of cars sold by them. For the salespeople, the program opens up the opportunity to be proactive when soliciting new business.

Sample Direct-Mail Letter

July 9, 1997

Dear Dr. _____:

Mark Twain once remarked, "Always do right. This will gratify some people and astonish the rest."

"Right" in this instance is (dealership name here) Motors' House Calls Program, through which you can gratify *and* astonish yourself. Your unique and important position automatically entitles you to have an exclusive, private demonstration of the (car model here) of your choice.

Our purpose is to give you an opportunity to evaluate, privately and of course without obligation, just how well suited to your needs the new (car model here) and the (dealership name here) support program are.

I will contact you soon to set a convenient time for you to enjoy this privilege at your office—or you may prefer I visit you at home.

Sincerely,

TABLE A.1. CALL/MARKETING RECORD

Prospect	Activity	Results
Name:	Letter sent:	
Address:	Call dates:	
Telephone:		

Prospect	Activity	Results
Name:	Letter sent:	
Address:	Call dates:	
Telephone:		

Prospect	Activity	Results
Name:	Letter sent:	
Address:	Call dates:	
Telephone:		

A Sample Multicall Work Plan

A major college textbook publisher decided to implement a teleselling campaign to provide coverage and increase sales at those schools that, because of size or sales volume, were not visited by an outside sales representative. In colleges, individual instructors usually select their own textbooks. However, in certain basic courses (for example, freshman composition, calculus, physics), it is not uncommon for a faculty committee to select the text. The approach adopted by the publisher illustrates both the power and reach of the telephone as a sales medium and also the benefit of integrating mail and telephone marketing into a complex, multicontact selling situation.

After careful study, sales management and the tellesellers decided to limit telemarketing coverage to seventy-five accounts (schools) in a territory during one of the four selling cycles into which the school year is divided (see the following schedule). The time spread of each cycle is tied both to the textbook selection decision date (when orders have to be at the school's bookstore[s]) and to the publication schedules of new books and revised editions of earlier books. The cycles, the products to be sold, and the marketing goals for each are as follows:

September–November	Sell new books published early (i.e., a 1997 book actually manufactured in the fall of 1996) and early new editions of previous books to professors using the previous edition.
November–January	Sell all books published (new, new editions, and existing) and available for shipment to all pro-

fessors teaching second-semester-only courses. Sell supplements (study guides and books of readings/cases) to all professors using a related main volume during the second semester.

February–March   For the following school year, sell all new books to all professors teaching the appropriate course, and, where an appropriate existing title was published, all professors teaching large-enrollment courses.

April–May   Sell all books to professors or schools that have late book-decision dates. Sell supplements to all professors in the territory who selected the main related volume.

With the preceding goals as guidelines, each teleseller is responsible for completing the following steps and calls in each selling cycle:

1. A sales letter is mailed to professors according to precall research that indicates there might be a potential sale. The letter states the purpose of the contact—interest in new textbooks, textbook needs for other courses, or an announcement of the publication of a new edition of a book—and invites a request for more information.

2. Those indicating interest are sent a descriptive brochure and another sales letter inviting recipients to call or write for a free copy of the book to examine closely for possible selection. Note is made at this point of all professors teaching large-enrollment courses who did not request an examination copy of the relevant textbook.

3. Those requesting an examination copy of the textbook are sent one immediately, along with a brief cover letter.

4. One week after the examination copies are sent, a telephone call is placed to the professors. This straight sales call is intended to get the professors to look inside the book, to make them aware of the features/advantages/benefits the book has, and to ask for the order (adoption).

5. If the book is selected at this time, appropriate follow-up is scheduled. If other selling work is required before the selection can be finalized (more information sent, copies of supplements provided, availability of test banks confirmed, and the like) additional sales calls are planned. All calls to a professor are made in anticipation of asking for the order.

6. A final sales letter follows the "ask for the order" call and, depending on whether or not the order is placed, has one of several goals. If no order is received, a final letter stresses anew the benefits of the book in question (and perhaps now includes a list of those schools that have already selected the textbook) and asks that it be seriously reconsidered. To professors who selected the company's textbook, a thank you letter, also promoting related supplements that can be ordered, is mailed and again followed by a telephone call to sell supplements.

7. If there is no response to Step 1 above from professors teaching large-enrollment courses, the telephone is once more employed, this time as a follow-up to learn why there was no response. This step can lead to resuming the cycle at Step 2 if the reason given for no response merits it (i.e., when the professor did not receive the letter, if a different professor has been assigned to teach the course, if no professor has yet been assigned to teach the course, and the like).

Some items of related interest are worthy of note:

1. *Record keeping.* Each teleseller tracks his schools for each cycle. Tracking is based on potential dollar volume to be closed in that cycle. As a result, for a given cycle the list of the seventy-five schools being contacted could vary from previous cycles. The tellesellers are in ongoing contact with all major schools in their territory, perhaps as many as 100 schools involving more than 1,000 professors.

2. *Work volume.* Each teleseller produces approximately 3,500 letters per year. With three tellesellers, such a flow of correspondence makes word-processing capability (an additional cost of teleselling) a must for the success of the operation. The letters are composed from a databank of prewritten paragraphs, arranged and customized on the instructions of the teleseller initiating the letter.

3. *Teleseller identity.* Heavy emphasis is placed on the teleseller's establishing her name in the minds of the prospects and customers, just as a field representative would do. Her business cards (with photograph), stationery, and note paper all let her contacts know who she is. Whenever possible, tellesellers are sent to staff company exhibits at academic conventions to allow further personal identification. It is estimated that the most successful of the tellesellers is known by as many as 300 instructors in his territory.

Straight A's

Report Card	
GRADE	SUBJECT
A	Approach
A	Analyze
A	Advocate
A	Answer
A	Ask
A	Apply

Sources for More Information

As with all professions, being a teleseller includes a lifetime learning requirement. Begin immediately to develop the habit of reading helpful books, listening to audio cassettes, and viewing related videotapes. The books, periodicals, and tapes listed here are devoted almost exclusively to teleselling. Your local librarian, bookseller, or audiovisual librarian can help you find others. But don't limit yourself to materials on teleselling. All salespeople share many common problems and situations and require similar skills. Any book, publication, or program on selling will be helpful, so long as you approach it with an open mind.

Books

Bencin, Richard. *Encyclopedia of Telemarketing*. Englewood Cliffs, NJ: Prentice-Hall, 1991.

Finch, Lloyd C. *Telephone Courtesy & Customer Service*, rev. ed.. Los Altos, CA: Crisp Publications, Inc., 1990.

Fisher, Peg. *Successful Telemarketing*. Chicago: Dartnell Corp., 1985.

Freestone, Julie, and Janet Brusse. *Telemarketing Basics: A Practical Guide for Professional Results*. Los Altos, CA: Crisp Publications, Inc., 1989.

Guiducci, Joan. *Power Calling: A Fresh Approach to Cold Calls & Prospecting*. Mill Valley, CA: Tonino, 1992.

Linchitz, Joel. *The Complete Guide to Telemarketing Management*. New York: AMACOM (American Management Association), 1990.

Masser, Barry Z. *Complete Handbook of All-Purpose Telemarketing Scripts*. Englewood Cliffs, NJ: Prentice-Hall, 1990.

Masser, Barry Z., and William M. Leeds. *Power Selling by Telephone*. Englewood Cliffs, NJ: Prentice-Hall, 1982.

Richardson, Linda. *Selling by Telephone: The Salesperson's Guide to Getting New Customers & Closing Deals*. New York: McGraw-Hill, 1992.

Sisk, Kathy. *Successful Telemarketing: The Complete Handbook on Managing a Profitable Telemarketing Call Center*. New York: McGraw-Hill, 1993.

Stone, Bob, and John Wyman. *Successful Telemarketing*. Lincolnwood, IL: NTC Business Books, 1991.

Magazines

Telemarketing®. One Technology Plaza, Norwalk, CT 06854, 800-243-6002 or 203-852-6800 (monthly).

TeleProfessional™: *Effective Marketing Via Telecommunications*. 209 West Fifth Street, Suite N, Waterloo, IA 50701-5420, 800-338-8307 or 319-235-9850 (ten issues per year).

Newsletters

Effective Telephone Techniques. Dartnell Corp., 4660 N. Ravenswood Avenue, Chicago, IL 60640-4510, 800-621-5463 or 312-561-4000.

Extensions. The Van Vechten Group, Ltd., 80 Scenic Drive, Suite 7, Freehold, NJ 07728-3478, 800-299-3499 or 908-780-5162 (every two weeks).

Professional Telephone Selling. Bureau of Business Practice, 24 Rope Ferry Road, Waterford, CT 06386, 800-876-9105 or 203-442-4365 (bimonthly).

Successful Telephone Selling. The Economics Press, 12 Daniel Road, Fairfield, NJ 07004-2575, 800-526-2554 or 201-227-1224 (every two weeks).

Telephone Selling Report. Business by Phone, Inc., 13254 Steven Street, Omaha, NE 68137-1728, 402-895-9399.

Audiocassettes

How to Be a Successful Telephone Sales Representative. American Management Association, 135 West 50th Street, New York, NY 10020, 800-262-9699.

Listen and Be Listened To. American Management Association, 135 West 50th Street, New York, NY 10020, 800-262-9699.

Sobczak, Art. *Ringing Up Sales*. Dartnell Corp., 4660 N. Ravenswood Avenue, Chicago, IL 60640-4510, 800-621-5463 or 312-561-4000.

Videocassettes

Alessandra, Tony. *The Power of Listening*. Dartnell Corp., 4660 N. Ravenswood Avenue, Chicago, IL 60640-4510, 800-621-5463 or 312-561-4000.

Effective Telephone Selling. Insight Media, 2162 Broadway, New York, NY 10024, 800-233-9910 or 212-721-6316.

New Telephone Talk: How to Deal with People over the Telephone. Salenger, 1635 12th Street, Santa Monica, CA 90404, 213-450-1300 (collect).

Sales Talk: Communication Styles. Insight Media, 2162 Broadway, New York, NY 10024, 800-233-9910 or 212-721-6316.

Scully, Robert. *Telemarketing.* D. E. Visuals, 3595 N.W. 83rd Avenue, Sunrise, FL 33351, 800-736-6438 or 305-741-6438.

Secrets of Telemarketing Scripts. Nimco, P.O. Box 9, 117 Hwy. 815, Calhoun, KY 42327-0009, 800-962-6662 or 502-273-5050.

Smith, Debra. *Professional Telephone Skills: Make Every Call More Positive and Productive.* CareerTrack Publications, 3085 Center Green Drive, P.O. Box 18778, Boulder, CO 80308-1778, 800-334-1018.

Telephone Skills: Courtesy on the Line. McGraw-Hill Training Systems, P.O. Box 641, Del Mar, CA 92014, 619-453-5000.

Other

Hello Direct®: Catalog of Telephone Productivity Tools. 5884 Eden Park Place, San Jose, CA 95138-1859, 800-444-3556.

Isaac, Steven. *Words for Telemarketing: How to Write Telephone Scripts for Maximum Results.* Caddylak Systems Inc., 201 Montrose Road, P.O. Box 1817, Westbury, NY 11590-1768, 800-523-8060.

And don't ignore books of a motivational nature: Napoleon Hill's *Think and Grow Rich*, Norman Vincent Peale's *The Power of Positive Thinking*, Anthony Robbins' *Awaken the Giant Within*, and the highly regarded *Born to Win* by Murial James and Dorothy Jongeward. These and others can help boost your ego and your sense of self-control. Books such as these can keep you on the track to continued success by equipping you with both the skills and the attitudes you need to be a winner.

Index

acceptance, as motive for buying, 25–26
accuracy, of information provided to prospects, 40
adaptive selling techniques, 129–140
  applying to different personal styles, 130, 135–140
  precautions about, 131
  social styles and, 131–135
advantages of product, 27, 29, 30, 32
  worksheets of, 169
advocating, 81–90
  body of presentation for, 88–89
  extemporaneously, 81–83
  opening statement for, 86–87, 186
  planned presentations for, 83–85
  script development for, 186
  transition statements for, 87–88
agreement
  with answer to objection, asking for, 100
  establishing pattern of, 76
Amiable-Sociable people, 134–135
  adapting to, 138
analogies, to get prospect's attention, 65
Analytical-Technical people, 135
  adapting to, 138–139
analyzing needs, 23–24, 69–80
  creating desires and, 72
  process for, 72–77

qualifying and. *See* qualifying prospects
  script development for, 186
anger. *See* hostility
answering complaints, 122–124
answering machines, 176
answering objections. *See* handling objections
answering questions
  closing an answer with a question and, 55–56
  script development for, 187
answering the telephone, courtesy for, 42, 121
antagonism. *See* hostility
apologizing
  to complaining customers, 124
  for taking up time, avoiding, 66
applying follow-up. *See* customer service; follow-up
appointments
  to avoid interruptions during calls, 170–171
  to call back, 175
appreciation, expressing, 42, 112, 115
approach, 62–68
  getting prospect's attention and, 62–67
  script development for, 185
arguing, avoiding, 100, 123
ask-a-question close, 110
asking for orders, 104–113
  ask-a-question close for, 110

asking for orders (*continued*)
    assume-the-order close for, 108
    buying signals and, 106–107
    choice close for, 109
    concluding calls after, 112
    fear of, 104–105
    learning techniques for, 111
    offer close for, 110
    ordering-instructions close for, 109
    refusals and. *See* refusals
    script development for, 187
    summation close for, 110–111
    timing of, 105–107
assertiveness, as social style, 131–132
assume-the-order close, 108
assumptions
    about anticipated objections, 95
    avoiding making, 73
attention
    comments to gain, 62–68
    questions to gain, 86
attire, 166
attitudes
    toward company and products, recognizing,
        146
    for listening, 161
    negative. *See* hostility; objections; refusals
    positive. *See* positive attitude
    state of, as barrier to communication,
        142–143
    survey of, 4–7
audio cassettes, list of, 208
authoritativeness
    in responding to complaints, 123–124
    in selling voice, 154

balance-sheet technique
    for closing, 111–112
    for handling objections, 100
belief in product, 16–17
benefits of product, 29, 31, 32
    buying of, 23
    of competitors' products, minimizing, 100
    mentioning in opening, 66

order of presenting, 76–77
for penetrating screens, 57
price as reflection of, 101–102
selling, 27
summarizing, 111–112
unique combination of, 85
words to convey, 148
worksheets of, 169
benefits of qualifying process, pointing out, 72
body of presentation, 88–89
books, list of, 207–208, 209
breaks, to avoid monotony, 179
building long-term relationships, 117–121
    information about customers needed for,
        118–120
    methods for, 120–121
business cards, 116
businesses
    identifying decision makers in, 55, 56, 57–58,
        71
    information needed for selling to, 53
    selling to, as purpose of calls, 53–54
buying decisions, 19–22
    considerations influencing, 20–22
    identifying people with authority to make,
        55, 56, 57–59, 71
buying motives. *See* motives for buying
buying recommendation, 88–89
    information needed to make, 71
buying signals, 106–107
    with assume-the-order close, 108

call binder, 166
call effectiveness, 31, 33
caller identification technology, 9
call flow and, strategy for, 16, 35–38, 45
call flow strategy, 16
calling back. *See* returning calls
calling plans, 54–55
call-routing equipment, 9
call screens. *See* screens
call strategy, 35–47. *See also* advocating;
        analyzing needs; answering questions;
        approach; asking for orders; follow-up;

handling objections; objections
   call flow and, 16, 35–38, 45
   for influencing prospects, 39–43
   listening and, 163
   objectives and, 73
   for product presentation, 16
   purpose of calls and, 43–45
   for qualifying, 73
card file, 54
challenging statements, in openings, 87
choice close, 109
closed questions, for qualifying prospects,
   75–76
closing
   on answers to objections, 100
   of sales. *See* asking for orders
clothing, 166
communication barriers, 141–147
   mental, 142, 144–145
   overcoming, 143–147
   personal, 142–143, 145–146
   physical, 143, 147
   verbal, 143, 146–147
competence, developing, 144–145
competitors
   avoiding criticism of, 100
   learning about, 77
complaint calls, 122–124
compliments, to get prospect's attention, 64
compromising, in handling complaints, 124
computers, 9–10, 166
concentration
   for listening, 160
   for overcoming communication barriers, 144,
     146
concluding statements, 112
confidence building, 144
congratulations, following close, 112
controls, 16
convenience, as motive for buying, 25
costs of selling methods, 10–11
courtesy, 41–43
   appropriate level of, 41–42, 43
   for incoming calls, 121–122

credibility
   establishing with prospects, 40
   voice and, 154
   word choice and, 149
credit cards, 9–10
criticism of competitors, avoiding, 100
cross-selling related products, 116
customers
   building relationships with. *See* building long-
     term relationships
   complaints from, 122–124
   follow-up with. *See* customer service; follow-up
   incoming calls from. *See* incoming calls
   keeping in touch with, 14
customer service
   for building long-term relationships, 120–121
   for incoming calls. *See* incoming calls
   information needed for, 118–120
   proactive, 117–121
   reasons for providing, 114
customizing form letters, 116

data sheets, 167
deadlines, for special offers, 101
decision makers, identifying, 56, 71
decisions. *See* buying decisions
defensiveness
   as barrier to communication, 142
   in handling objections, 95
demonstrations, 150
desires. *See also* analyzing needs; needs
   analyzing, 23–24
   creating, 72
   insufficient for sale, 93
diary, for follow-up, 120
direct-mail marketing, costs of, 10
discount pricing strategy, 101
disqualifying factors, 73–74
distractions. *See also* interruptions
   as barriers to communication, 142
dramatic statements, in openings, 87
dressing for work, 166
Driven-Dominant people, 133–134
   adapting to, 136–138

effective calls, 31, 33
emotional considerations, in buying decision, 21
empathy, for overcoming communication
     barriers, 146
enthusiasm, 89
     conveying, 66–67, 149
     for handling objections, 100
     for listening, 161–162
expertise, creating impression of, 71
Expressive-Extroverted people, 134
     adapting to, 137
expressiveness, of selling voice, 154
extemporaneous presentations
     for advocating, 81–83
     avoiding in openings, 63
     benefits of, 82

false objections, 94, 99
fear
     of asking for orders, 104–105
     as motive for buying, 25
     of rejection, 105
features of product, 27, 28, 30, 32
     worksheets of, 169
files
     of data sheets, 167
     work diary and, 167–168
financial gain, as motive for buying, 24
flip chart, 166
flow pattern, of sales calls, 35–38
     strategy for, 16, 35–38, 45
follow-up, 13, 52, 114–128. *See also* customer
     service
     benefits of, 116–117
     on complaints, 124
     with existing accounts, 14
     on literature sent to prospect, 65, 116
     mailings for, 115–116
     organization for, 115
     script development for, 187–188
     setting up opportunities for, 111–112
     timing of, 117
form letters, customizing, 116

friendliness, overdoing, 153
frivolous comments, during opening, 66

goals
     of calls, 44, 53–54
     for number of calls, 174
grammar, 151
guarantees, 110

habit, objecting as, 92
handling objections, 96–101
     answering objections and, 99–100
     balance-sheet technique for, 100
     during closings, 111
     confirming understanding of objection for, 99
     defensiveness in, 95
     enthusiasm for, 100
     to large inventory, 98
     Objections Handbook for, 96
     positive attitude for, 100
     preparation for, 98
     to price, 98, 101–102
     qualifying objections for, 99
     to recent purchase, 98
     restatement for, 99, 101
     script development for, 187
     special offers for, 100–101
     before they are voiced, 94–95
     timing of, 95
     word choice for, 100
hanging up, timing of, 42, 122
hard offers, 92
hearing, listening compared with, 158
hostility, 179–180
     of callers, handling, 122–124
     in selling voice, 153

image. *See* impressions
impatience
     avoiding when answering calls, 122
     of prospect, with qualifying process, 72
impressions
     of expertise, 71

formation of, 63
made on prospects, 40–41
incoming calls, 121–127
answering promptly, 121
complaint calls, 122–124
courtesy for, 121–122
returning, 126–127
taking messages and, 122, 124–126
individuals as customers
identifying decision makers and, 58–59
information needed for selling to, 53
selling to, as purpose of calls, 53
industry phraseology, 151
industry problems, basing openings on, 65
influencing prospects, 39–43
courtesy for, 41–43
credibility for, 40
demonstrating interest in prospect for, 39
impressions and, 40–41
speech habits and, 40
information
about complaints, 123
about prospects, sources of, 54
about teleselling, sources of, 207–209
accuracy of, 40
information needs
for building long-term relationships, 118–120
for qualifying prospects, 74, 77–79
for selling to businesses, 53
for selling to individuals, 53
initial benefit statement (IBS), 66
interest in prospect, demonstrating, 39, 122
word choice for, 148
International Periodicals Directory, 50
interruptions
avoiding interrupting incoming calls and, 122, 123
avoiding interrupting prospects and, 160
with Dominant-Driven people, 136–137
making appointments with prospects to avoid, 170–171
irate calls, handling, 122–124

jargon, 150–151
joking, during opening, 66

keyboard, 166
knock-out factors, in qualifying, 73–74
knowledge of product. *See* product knowledge

large inventory objection, handling, 98
lead-in statements, 65
leads
definition of, 13
qualifying, 13
length of calls, 172–173, 174–175
letters. *See also* mailings
customizing, 116
listening, 156–164
avoiding interruptions and, 160
to complaints, 123
concentrating and, 160
emphasis on, 17
enthusiasm and, 161–162
evaluating effectiveness of, 158–159
hearing compared with, 158
importance of, 156–158
keeping an open mind and, 161
to learn about market and competitors, 77
by prospect, encouraging, 63
for prospect's point of view, 107
for qualifying prospects, 76, 77
for selling opportunities, 162–163
staying fresh and, 161
literature. *See* mailings
long-term relationships, building. *See* building long-term relationships

magazines, list of, 208
mailing lists, 50, 51–52
mailings
costs of direct-mail marketing and, 10
customizing, 116
following up on, 65
for follow-up, 115–116
sample mail-and-phone program and, 199–202

mailings (*continued*)
    sending before call, 150
managing calls, 171–176
    answering machines and, 176
    appointments for calling back and, 175
    length of calls and, 172–173, 174–175
    making appointments with prospects to avoid
        interruptions and, 170–171
    number of calls per day and, 171–172, 174
    timing of calls and, 175
manners. *See* courtesy
market, learning about, 77
mental barriers to communication, 142
    overcoming, 144–145
messages
    informing caller about callback system and,
        126
    leaving on answering machines, 176
    routing to intended recipient, 125–126
    taking from callers, 122, 124–126
mistakes, objections resulting from, 93
misunderstandings
    confirming understanding of objection to
        avoid, 99
    objections resulting from, 93–94, 101
    word choice and, 151
money, as motive for buying, 24
monotone, overcoming, 153, 154
monotony, handling, 178–179
mood, as barrier to communication, 142
motives for buying, 22–26
    acceptance and respect as, 25–26
    benefits and, 23
    convenience as, 25
    fear as, 25
    financial gain as, 24
    needs and desires and, 23–24
    pleasure as, 25
    satisfying, 26
    security as, 24–25
    sex appeal as, 25

names
    using in calls, 42, 57, 122

using when answering telephone, 121
neatness, of mailings, 116
needs. *See also* desires
    analyzing. *See* analyzing needs; qualifying
        prospects
    building sense of, 57
    for information. *See* information needs
    insufficient, 93
    summarizing, 86, 111–112
nervousness, as barrier to communication, 142
newsletters, list of, 208
note taking, 158

objections, 91–103
    false, 94, 99
    handling. *See* handling objections
    heading off, 94–95
    misunderstandings as, 93–94
    pressuring prospects as cause of, 108
    real, 94
    reasons for, 92–93
    stalls, 93, 99
    stimulating, 107
    timing of, 92, 95
Objections Handbook, 96
objectives
    for call, 171
    call strategy and, 73
    need to establish, 16
offer close, 110
open-ended questions, for qualifying prospects,
    75
openings, 62–68
    in advocating, 86–87
    making businesslike, 66
    planning, 63
order, of presenting benefits, 76–77
ordering-instructions close, 109
orders
    asking for. *See* asking for orders
    follow-up on, 120
    maintaining contact between, 116
    refusal to place. *See* refusals
organization, 165–171

data sheets for, 167
for follow-up, 115
preparing prospects and, 170–171
sales kit for, 168–170
work diary for, 167–168
outside sales visits, costs of, 10

paperwork, organizing, 115
payment, determining prospect's ability to pay and, 71
performance. *See* productivity
personal barriers to communication, 142–143
    overcoming, 145–146
personal items, in work space, 166
physical barriers to communication, 143
    overcoming, 147
planning
    calling plans and, 54–55
    of openings, 63
    of presentations, 83–85. *See also* scripts
    sample work plan and, 203–205
pleasure, as motive for buying, 25
politeness. *See* courtesy
positive attitude, 176–180
    handling monotony and, 178–179
    for handling objections, 100
    hostile people and, 179–180
    self-selling and, 177–178
    toward telephone, 177
    tracking results to maintain, 177
positive words, 148–150
practice, to develop competence, 144–145
precision, of words, 150
preemptive statements, for heading off objections, 94–95
prejudices, overcoming, 161
premiums, for buying, 100–101
preparation
    for handling objections, 98
    for overcoming communication barriers, 147
    of prospects, 170–171
pressuring prospects, avoiding, 108
price
    discount pricing strategy and, 101

as reflection of value received, 101–102
price objection, 101–102
    handling, 98
problems, complaints about, 122–124
product
    advocating. *See* advocating
    belief in, 16–17
    benefits of. *See* benefits of product
    cross-selling, 116
    enthusiasm about. *See* enthusiasm
    features of, 27, 28, 30, 32
    questions to build interest in, 71
    relating to comments of authorities, 66
    strategy for presentation of, 16
    transition to presentation of, 87–88
    words to describe, 149–150
productivity
    evaluating, 59
    managing calls for. *See* managing calls
    performance evaluation survey for, 193–196
    tracking to maintain a positive attitude, 177
product knowledge, 27–33
    about advantages, 27, 29, 30, 32
    about benefits, 29, 31, 32
    about features, 27, 28, 30, 32
    benefits of, 33
    demonstrating to prospect, 65
    getting across in calls, 31, 33
product recommendation, 88–89
    information needed to make, 71
professionalism, of mailings, 116
promptness, of returning calls, 126, 127
prospecting, 48–61
    calling plan for, 54–55
    calling problems in, 55–57
    identifying decision makers and, 57–59
    identifying prospects and, 51–52
    information for, 54
    narrowing the universe and, 49–51
    potential numbers of prospects and, 49
    precall research for, 53–54
    productivity and, 59
prospects
    arguing with, avoiding, 100

prospects (*continued*)
  buying signals from. *See* buying signals
  cues to ineffective listening from, 158–159
  determining ability to pay, 71
  encouraging interaction from, 76
  establishing pattern of agreement by, 76
  getting attention of, 62–68, 86
  influencing, 39–43
  interest in. *See* interest in prospect, demon-
    strating
  matching rate of speech to, 136, 153
  matching word choice to, 150
  not wanting unsolicited calls, 175–176
  preparing, 170–171
  pressuring, avoiding, 108
  providing rationalizations for, 22
  qualified, 49
  qualifying. *See* qualifying prospects
  screening, 16
  social styles of. *See* social styles
  using name of, 42, 57
putting calls on hold, 42

qualified prospects, 49
qualifying leads, 13
qualifying objections, 99
qualifying prospects, 70–71, 74–77
  analyzing needs and. *See* analyzing needs
  closed questions for, 75–76
  listening for, 76, 77
  open-ended questions for, 75
  prospect's impatience with, 72
  reasons for, 70–71
  using available data for, 74
qualifying suspects, 50–51
questions
  about complaints, 123
  answering. *See* answering questions
  ask-a-question close and, 110
  to build interest, 71, 86
  closed, 75–76
  to create desire to buy, 72
  to encourage interaction, 76

to get prospect's attention, 64
open-ended, 75
for qualifying prospects, 75–76, 78–79
to summarize needs, 86

random dialers, 9
rapport, building, 17
rate of speech. *See* speech rate
rational considerations, in buying decision,
    20–21
rationalizations
  in buying decision, 21–22
  providing, 22
real objections, 94
recent purchase objection, handling, 98
record keeping
  call binder and, 166
  data sheets and, 167
  organizing, 115
  work diary and, 167–168
referrals, asking for, 112
refusals
  fear of, 104–105
  learning not to take personally, 123
  responding to, 107
  setting up opportunity to call back and,
    111–112
rejection, 49. *See also* refusals
relaxation, for overcoming communication
    barriers, 146
research, precall, 53–54
respect, as motive for buying, 25–26
responsiveness, as social style, 132–133
restatement
  of complaints, 123
  of objections, 99, 101
resupplying, 116–117
returning calls, 126–127
  appointments for, 175
  informing callers about callback system and,
    126
rigidity, as reason for objections, 92
risk avoidance, as reason for objections, 92

sales, volume of, 9–10
sales kit, 168–170
sales literature. *See* mailings
salespeople
    general skills needed by, 16–17
    supporting, 13–14
    teleselling skills needed by, 17–18
samples, sending before call, 150
screening prospects, 16
screens, 55–57
    getting around, 55–56
    going above, 56–57
    going below, 56
    working through, 57
scripts, 63, 182–192
    advantages of, 183
    developing, 185–188
    disadvantages of, 184
    examples of, 188–192
    working without. *See* extemporaneous
      presentations
security, as motive for buying, 24–25
self-selling list, 177–178
selling methods, costs of, 10–11
selling opportunities, listening for, 162–163
selling voice, 40, 89, 151–154
    antagonism in, 153
    authoritativeness in, 154
    distinctness of, 154
    evaluating, 151–152
    expressive, 154
    friendliness in, 153
    monotone and, 153, 154
    naturalness of, 154
    rate of speech and. *See* speech rate
    sincerity in, 153
sentence construction, 151
service. *See* customer service; incoming calls
sex appeal, as motive for buying, 25
sincerity, in selling voice, 153
skills
    general, for salespeople, 16–17
    survey of, 4–7

for telesellers, 17–18
social styles
    adapting to, 130, 135–140
    Amiable-Sociable, 134–135, 138
    Analytical-Technical, 135, 138–139
    assertive, 131–132
    clues to, 131, 133–135
    Driven-Dominant, 133–134, 136–138
    Expressive-Extroverted, 134, 137
    responsive, 132–133
soft offers, 92, 110
special-interest-publication subscriber lists, 50
special offers, 100–101
speech habits, 40. *See also* selling voice; speech
    rate; verbal barriers to communication;
    voice; word choice
speech rate, 40, 89, 153
    complaint calls and, 123
    matching, 122, 136, 153
stalls, 93, 99
The Standard Industrial Classification Manual,
    50
Standard Industrial Classification (SIC) num-
    bers, 50
statements
    challenging, in openings, 87
    concluding, 112
    dramatic, in openings, 87
    to get prospect's attention, 64, 65, 87
    initial benefit statement, 66
    lead-in, 65
    opening, 86–87, 186
    preemptive, for heading off objections, 94–95
    transitional, 87–88
strategies
    for call. *See* advocating; analyzing needs;
      answering questions; approach; asking for
      orders; call strategy; follow-up; handling
      objections; objections
    for prospecting, 54–59
summation close, 111–112
superlatives, avoiding, 149
supporting salespeople, 13–14

surprise, in teleselling, 17
suspects, 49
   identifying, 50
   qualifying, 50–51

taking messages, 122, 124–126
targeting, 12
technology
   computer, 9–10
   telephone, 8–9
teleblitz, number of calls and, 174
telephone, 8–12, 166
   attitude toward, 177
   cost savings using, 10–11
   as primary instrument for selling, 14–15
   technology for, 8–9
   time savings using, 11–12
teleselling, definition of, 15–16
thanks, expressing, 42, 112, 115
third-party references, to get prospect's attention, 65
time
   constraints on, 16–17
   saving using telephone, 11–12
timing
   of asking for orders, 105–107
   of calls, 175
   of follow-up, 116, 117
   of handling objections, 95
   of hanging up, 42, 122
   of mailings, 116
   of objections, 92, 95
   to penetrate screens, 56
   of returning calls, 126–127
transition statements, 87–88

urgency, building sense of, 57

variety, to avoid monotony, 179
verbal barriers to communication, 143. *See also* selling voice; voice; word choice
   overcoming, 146–147
video cassettes, list of, 208–209
voice
   of Amiable-Sociable people, 134
   of Analytical-Technical people, 135
   of Driven-Dominant people, 133
   of Expressive-Extroverted people, 134
   selling. *See* selling voice

WATS (Wide Area Telephone Service) lines, 8–9
Weekly Progress Report, 57
word choice, 16–17, 40, 89, 147–151
   for adaptive selling, 136
   believability and, 149
   to convey benefits, 148
   to convey enthusiasm, 149
   to demonstrate interest, 148
   to describe products, 149–150
   of Driven-Dominant people, 133
   grammar and sentence construction and, 151
   for handling complaints, 123
   for handling objections, 100
   industry phraseology and, 151
   jargon and, 150–151
   matching to prospect's terms, 150
   positive words and, 148–150
   precision of, 150
work diary, 167–168
work plan, sample, 203–205
work space, organizing, 165–166
worrying, as barrier to communication, 142